RED, WHITE, AND BLACK

Rescuing American History
from Revisionists and Race Hustlers

ROBERT L. WOODSON SR., EDITOR

EMANCIPATION
BOOKS

AN EMANCIPATION BOOK
An Imprint of Post Hill Press
ISBN: 978-1-63758-261-9

Red, White, and Black:
Rescuing American History from Revisionists and Race Hustlers
© 2021 by Robert L. Woodson Sr., Editor
All Rights Reserved
First Emancipation Books Hardcover Edition: May 2021

Cover Design by Tiffani Shea

Post Hill Press
New York • Nashville
posthillpress.com

Published in the United States of America
1 2 3 4 5 6 7 8 9 10

"Their statesmanship looked beyond the passing moment, and stretched away in strength into the distant future. They seized upon eternal principles, and set a glorious example in their defense. Mark them!"

—Frederick Douglass, referring to the Founding Fathers in his speech "The Meaning of July Fourth for the Negro," delivered in Rochester, New York, on July 5, 1852.

DEDICATION

No nation is perfect, but America—more than any other—is a place where people from every imaginable background have been able to pursue their dreams and realize their potential. Americans have never met a problem we are afraid to tackle or a challenge we can't overcome. In fact, those of us who have faced the most formidable challenges in life often become our strongest leaders and our greatest patriots.

This is as true of black Americans as it is anyone else. During the worst of Jim Crow, we built thriving communities full of families, churches, businesses, and countless civic institutions. On the very soil where we once toiled in forced labor, we found the seeds of our liberation.

At a time when many are trying to pull us apart by stoking grievances and sowing discord, the overwhelming majority of Americans remain devoted to our founding principles and to one another. This book is dedicated to those countless millions who love our country, despite its flaws, and long to live together in peace.

1776 UNITES
MISSION STATEMENT

1776 Unites is a movement to liberate tens of millions of Americans by helping them become agents of their own uplift and transformation, by embracing the true founding values of our country. 1776 Unites represents a nonpartisan and intellectually diverse alliance of hundreds of thousands of writers, thinkers, and activists focused on solutions to our country's greatest challenges in education, culture, and upward mobility.

We acknowledge that racial discrimination exists—and work towards diminishing it. But we <u>dissent from contemporary groupthink and rhetoric about race, class, and American history</u> that defames our national heritage, divides our people, and instills helplessness among those who already hold within themselves the grit and resilience to better their lot in life. 1776 Unites maintains a special focus on voices in the black community who celebrate black excellence and reject victimhood culture and showcases the millions of black Americans who have prospered by embracing the founding ideals of America.

We are intellectuals and journalists, entrepreneurs and grassroots activists, celebrating the progress America has made, the resilience of its people, and our future together. We seek decisive action in restoring our people's confidence and advancing the cause of *actual* justice in the face of hostile messages that degrade the spiritual, moral, and political foundations of our nation.

1776 Unites is a project of the Woodson Center, a community transformation and empowerment organization founded by Robert L. Woodson Sr. in 1981.

CONTENTS

FOREWORD
BY DR. LUCAS E. MOREL

"It should never be lost sight of, that our destiny for good or for evil, for time and for eternity, is, by an all-wise God, committed to us; and that all the helps or hindrances with which we may meet on earth, can never release us from this high and heaven-imposed responsibility."

—Frederick Douglass (1848)[1]

"Always bear in mind that your own resolution to succeed, is more important than any other one thing."

—Abraham Lincoln (1855)[2]

Frederick Douglass and Abraham Lincoln would smile upon this book of essays. Both men exuded the Spirit of '76 and, like the essays herein, sought to reclaim the noble ideals of the Declaration of Independence to meet the challenges of their times. Each knew of the landing of Africans near Jamestown, Virginia, in 1619, and the significance of this introduction of African slavery onto American soil.[3] However, neither saw that event as equivalent to, let alone surpassing, what Americans have long believed marked America's *Novus ordo seclorum*, or "new order of the ages"—namely, when thirteen American colonies-turned-states declared their independence on July 4, 1776. Douglass and Lincoln identified that date as *the* American Founding because it not only announced a break from Great Britain but also expressed a universal, transcendent foundation for legitimate government.[4] In the spirit of these two champions of the timeless truths of the Declaration, 1776 Unites argues that those truths constitute the surest basis for individual prosperity and the key to reuniting a country divided over the role that race should play in its social and political life.

In the essays that follow, while hindrances are acknowledged, the authors focus on what black Americans have the power to do for themselves, their neighbors, and their country. Frederick Douglass never denied that white Americans needed to remove "the barriers to our improvement, which themselves have set up," but he consistently emphasized that "the main work must be commenced, must be carried on, and concluded by ourselves."[5] He exhorted black Americans to cultivate character above all else. It not only elevated a man but also helped to undercut color prejudice against him.

This required a moral effort on the part of black people precisely because it was required of all people. The key to liberation, Douglass never tired of proclaiming, lay within each person. To be sure, government has a role to play, but even the most robust efforts by government to protect the citizenry would avail them little if they themselves did not use their freedom to develop their natural human capacity. This has always been the purpose of education, and the essays in *Red, White, and Black* illustrate many essential ways that appealing to the minds and hearts of black people, and not to their color, offers the formula for success.

This book also points to the role that faith plays in giving hope to those who face obstacles. Faith in God played a pivotal role in the civil rights struggle, marking the manifest contributions to peaceful progress by leaders such as Martin Luther King Jr., Rosa Parks, John Lewis, and Mahalia Jackson. Christian virtues like forgiveness, perseverance, and most of all *agape* love were instrumental in avoiding the bloodshed of race wars that could have occurred but for the abiding restraint of so many black Americans. Their belief in revealed, transcendent truths jibes well with the natural, transcendent principles that constitute the Spirit of '76.

Importantly, the task of black American liberation and self-government had to begin even *before* prejudices were conquered and barriers were removed. Black Americans have always fought for their rights even before the elimination of discriminatory laws and practices. In fact, one might describe American history as one long civil rights movement, where a diverse people and their government developed by fits and starts in their march towards securing freedom and equality for all.[6] In so believing and doing, black Americans may count themselves no less the sons and daughters of the American Revolution than the literal descendants of the generation that fought to establish a country on the basis of equality, liberty, and government by consent of the governed.

Lincoln once explained that these concepts, at once distinctively American and profoundly universal, were the inheritance of every citizen of the United States. Speaking of immigrants to the United States, he noted that while they could not trace their bloodline to the fathers of the American republic, "when they look through that old Declaration of Independence they find that those old men say that 'We hold these truths to be self-evident, that all men are created equal,' and then they feel that that moral sentiment taught in that day evidences their relation to those men, that it is the father of all moral principle in them, and that they have a right to claim it as though they were blood of the blood, and flesh of the flesh of the men who wrote that Declaration, and so they are."[7] The stories told in *Red, White, and Black* echo Lincoln's sentiment, claiming the principles of the

Declaration for all black Americans—"and so they are." In this way, the Spirit of '76 unifies because it embraces all humanity.

An essential theme of these essays is the importance of the individual as contrasted with the more popular emphasis upon group identity. One of the grand ironies of today's "identity politics" is that the solidarity or collective mindset promoted by appeals to race pride ignores the *individual* identities of those it claims to elevate. Moreover, it also neglects or downplays the *diversity* of each individual, whose true identity could never be summed up by reference only to race (or any other attribute). In doing so, today's racial identity mongers undermine substantive advancement of racial minorities by not calling forth their individual efforts to develop their natural capacity for self-government.

In addition, identity politics diverts government away from protecting what Martin Luther King Jr. called "citizenship rights" and towards distributing benefits and burdens on the basis of membership in protected groups.[8] Douglass noted, "I know of no rights of race superior to the rights of humanity." A steadfast believer in equality under the law, he insisted that the "Constitution knows no man by the color of his skin" and therefore did not believe race should be the measure of anyone's constitutional rights.[9]

In this focus upon his rights as an American citizen and not as a black man, Douglass foreshadowed Justice Louis Harlan's famous, lone dissenting opinion in the infamous 1896 *Plessy v. Ferguson* case, which produced the insidious doctrine of "separate but equal." Harlan wrote, "Our Constitution is color-blind, and neither knows nor tolerates classes among citizens. In respect of civil rights, all citizens are equal before the law."[10] Unfortunately, Harlan's dissent was outnumbered by seven other justices who interpreted the Fourteenth Amendment to allow states to segregate citizens according to their racial identity as long as they did so equally. Subsequent Supreme Court cases have ratcheted up the standard of judicial scrutiny of racial classifications and, in the 1954 case of *Brown v. Board of Education of Topeka, Kansas,* finally ruled that racial segregation was unconstitutional.[11] However, a majority of the high court has never interpreted the Constitution to be color-blind. Racial identity remains a permissible way for government to include some citizens and exclude others when providing opportunities, like admission to the nation's colleges and universities or securing government jobs and contracts.[12] With the Court endorsing racial identity as a "plus," at least for some citizens, it's no surprise that seeking advancement through group identity continues to offer an alluring path for some black Americans.

Douglass argued that cultivating "race pride" was actually "a positive evil." By offering no basis for tangible, practical accomplishments, he looked upon the enterprise as "building on a false foundation." He reminded fellow black Americans that the color prejudice at the root of slavery, segregation, and the manifold discrimination they faced—what he termed "American race pride"—was precisely the result of "an assumption of superiority upon the ground of race and color" and the very "thing we are fighting against." He added, "Do we not know that every argument we make, and every pretension we set up in favor of race pride, is giving the enemy a stick to break our own heads?"[13] If they had been discriminated against in the past, the way forward was not discrimination in their favor but equal protection of the laws—what they were owed all along.

Douglass also reminded his black readers, "Our race and color are not of our own choosing. We have no volition in the case one way or another." He, therefore, thought it "ridiculous" that someone would want to take credit for "the gift of the Almighty."[14] An appeal to group pride without also exhorting members of the group to conduct befitting a free person amounts to nothing more than a pose and therefore a vain exercise that promotes self-esteem without requiring any effort.

For the better part of American history, black Americans wanted nothing to do with a color line that separated them from the rest of the American population. Douglass wrote that it was "our enemies" who sought "to deepen and widen the line of separation between the white and colored people of this country." Given that blacks were a numerical minority in the United States, color had never been a help to them. What Douglass learned from the American Founders, including slaveholders like Washington, Jefferson, and Madison, was that the only relevant minority in America was the minority of one—the individual. In Douglass's words, "color should not be a criterion of rights."[15]

To the extent that blacks seek security in their citizenship as Americans rather than the color of their skin, they strengthen their just claims under the Constitution. During the Civil War, Douglass devoted himself to getting white Americans "to trust the operation of their own principles."[16] Once the war concluded, he maintained that his goal was "to make our government entirely consistent with itself."[17] Simply put, Douglass thought the government of all should be partial to none, and thereby leave each person responsible for the exercise of his or her liberties. Under a government that protects all citizens equally and that operates according to their consent, all can now rise or fall according to their respective efforts.

Black Americans throughout our history expressed the best in American ideals when they strove against the odds to overcome unjust obstacles to make a meaningful life for themselves in the United States. Similarly, the generation that fought in the Revolutionary War acted like a free people even before their independence was secured. As one of the main draftsmen of the Declaration of Independence, John Adams, wrote, "The Revolution was effected before the War commenced. The Revolution was in the Minds and Hearts of the people."[18]

Frederick Douglass demonstrated this same mindset even while legally still a slave when he resisted the beating of a slave breaker: "I had reached the point, at which *I was not afraid to die.* This spirit made me a freeman in *fact,* while I remained a slave in *form.*"[19] Douglass took the measure of his oppressive circumstances, and most especially of his God-given capacity as a human being, and determined not to remain a victim of his environment. Douglass called it the "turning-point" of his "career as a slave" when he resolved that, "however long I might remain a slave in form, the day had passed forever when I could be a slave in fact."[20] He would pursue his own liberation, and that of his fellow bondsmen, eventually making a career of reminding fellow Americans of the ideals of the Declaration of Independence and the protections of the Constitution.

But these founding documents are now under suspicion, if not flat-out attack. Americans have forgotten how they are connected to the Founding. This civic identity crisis is most evident in current discussions and strife involving race. Americans have begun to believe that the continuance of slavery by the leading statesmen of that era demonstrates that our revolutionary fathers did not believe that all men were included when they wrote in the Declaration of Independence "that all men are created equal." As the greatest defender of the American Founding, even Lincoln is included among the targets of those who see racism at worst, and hypocrisy at best, in the most iconic political figures of eighteenth- and nineteenth-century America.[21]

Without question Exhibit A is the hullabaloo over the 1619 Project. Curated by Nikole Hannah-Jones, the *New York Times* Magazine devoted its entire issue on August 18, 2019, to essays and art inspired by the notion that 1619 was the real founding of America because of the introduction of African slaves at Point Comfort, near the English colony of Jamestown. Its lead essay by Ms. Hannah-Jones argued that racial slavery planted so early in the American continent infected the development of the eventual nation's society and politics as to engender anti-black racism that "runs in the very DNA of this country."[22]

Her thesis and related essays under the auspices of the 1619 Project have received serious criticism that can readily be found online and in print. Suffice it to say, historians, political scientists, and economists from across the political spectrum have weighed the 1619 Project and found it seriously wanting in terms of its scholarship. I found Hannah-Jones's essay not only deficient in its understanding of both Lincoln and the American Founding, but also politically divisive in its presentation of American history as heroic black virtue triumphing over persistent white vice.[23] The short shrift she pays to the goodwill of so many white citizens who supported the individual and collective black freedom struggle can only sap the trust that is necessary for racial diversity to strengthen rather than weaken our national union.

In the end, what do America's youth, especially those of color, need to equip themselves for success? What can they start doing today, even in the face of lingering prejudice, to put them on the path to both material and spiritual well-being? These essays in *Red, White, and Black* brim with the agency, initiative, and aspiration of ordinary black Americans, telling stories that inspire precisely because they illustrate the success within any American's reach, if only he or she believes. America's promise, the Spirit of '76, remains "the ring-bolt to the chain of your nation's destiny," Douglass told us, because it holds the greatest potential to liberate all who strive to fulfill it, as well as once again unite us as one American people.

INTRODUCTION:
THE CRUCIAL VOICE OF "1776"
BY ROBERT L. WOODSON SR.

While the country's chatting classes had their attention riveted on the impeachment of the president and the national elections that took place in 2020, the moral ground under our feet was shaking with small seismic tremors that portend a major eruption that could tear this country apart. As those who promote identity politics fan the flames of animosity and thrive on division, our nation is breaking apart.

One of the most virulent and volatile areas of division is race. The purveyors of animosity have fine-tuned their strategy on this issue, creating a villain composed of "white privilege" and "institutional racism" that must be countered through a game plan of entitlements and reparations for its victims. The grand weapon in this warfare is the 1619 Project, launched by the *New York Times* in a one hundred-page insert of a collection of writings. These writings postulate that the "actual" founding of America occurred in 1619 with the arrival of the first slaves on our nation's shores and declare that America is essentially and irrevocably rooted in injustice and racism.

The weight of the legacy of slavery and Jim Crow laws is said to be the cause of any and all racial disparity that exists today and is declared the source of the devastation of crime-ridden, predominantly black inner cities and skyrocketing homicides, as well as the dissolution of families and communities. To counter the debilitating and dangerous message of the 1619 Project, we are launching 1776 Unites, honoring the vision of our nation's Founders, who saw beyond their years. Though slavery and discrimination undeniably are a tragic part of our nation's history, we have made strides along its long and tortuous journey to realize its promise and abide by its founding principles. People are motivated to achieve and overcome the challenges that confront them when they learn about inspiring victories that are possible and are not barraged by constant reminders of injuries they have suffered.

In truth, even during the times of the worst oppression, there were blacks who were in slavery but not *of slavery*—who maintained a strong moral code and a belief in self-determination and mutual support that allowed them to rise. A surprising number of black men and women who were born slaves died as millionaires. Even in the era of legislated segregation and discrimination, blacks tapped an entrepreneurial legacy to launch thriving enterprises, including hotels, banks, hospitals, dental schools, insurance companies, and a railroad. In fact, the black business district of Durham, North Carolina, was widely known as "Black Wall Street."

Another famous black entrepreneurial enclave was the Greenwood section of Tulsa, Oklahoma. When oil was discovered in Tulsa in the early 1900s, the city underwent an enormous growth spurt. Though African Americans were not allowed to create business ventures in the major district and were not even welcomed as customers in the white business district, rather than taking service jobs and doing domestic service labor for others, many adventurous blacks chose to develop their own business district. By 1921, the business enclave had developed into an impressive array of enterprises.

Tragically, in that year, a young black delivery man was falsely accused of attacking a white woman. Tensions rose and erupted into chaos as a mob of angry whites looted stores, shot at blacks in the streets, and torched businesses, homes, and churches. In this violence, 860 African American businesses and homes were destroyed and, afterward, the Greenwood business section lay in ruins. Undaunted, and displaying the same entrepreneurial spirit that initially built the Greenwood section, blacks joined together in a massive effort of rebuilding. By 1938, business enterprises and community organizations once again anchored the community. This spectrum of achievement is a powerful refutation of the claim that the destiny of black Americans is determined by what whites do—or what they have done in the past.

Until the 1960s, poverty did not entail social dysfunction in the black community. In ten years of the Depression, when the United States overall had a negative GNP and a nearly 25 percent unemployment rate, the unemployment rate in the black community was over 40 percent. Even then, the marriage rate in the black community was higher than it was in the white community, despite times of economic deprivation and racism. In 1925 in New York City, 85 percent[24] of black families were a husband and wife raising their children—while today the rate of out-of-wedlock births among blacks has skyrocketed to nearly 71 percent.[25]

In his book, *The Future Once Happened Here*, historian Fred Siegel explains that radical, liberal social activists in the 1960s concluded that one way to reveal the moral shortcomings of capitalism was to flood the system with welfare recipients. In detaching work from income, and thereby diminishing men and the role they played as fathers, welfare dependency, drug addiction, and school dropouts would increase, ultimately "opening [the nation up] to radical change."[26] These policies, espoused by Columbia University professors Richard Cloward, Frances Fox Piven, and others, were followed by government action to actually recruit people into the welfare system. These efforts lifted the stigma of welfare as social insurance and replaced it with the idea of "welfare rights," and in the case of blacks, replaced it with the idea of reparations.[27] Thus the black family and other families began to decline, followed by out-of-wedlock births and poverty. Prior to this time, even in the face of Jim Crow laws, legalized discrimination, and a lack of voting rights, the black community did not experience the wide-scale despair and destruction that we witness today because of a strong Christian moral code of conduct, a conviction in self-determination and mutual assistance, and strong families and communities.

We are launching 1776 Unites to counter the false history that the 1619 Project espouses and has disseminated as a school curriculum. We aim to highlight the victories that are possible in spite of oppression, and to open the door to discussion of solutions to the moral disarray that afflicts not only minority, low-income neighborhoods but also takes its toll among the sons and daughters of the affluent. In Palo Alto, California, where two-parent, highly educated households predominate, the suicide rate among teenagers is six times the national average.[28] Drug addiction among affluent, white youths in New Hampshire is dramatically rising.[29]

Throughout America, we are witnessing the widespread self-destruction and devastation that is the consequence of the perversion of the values that once united us and protected us from both internal and external enemies. As Samuel Adams presciently warned, "A dissolution of principles and manners will more surely overthrow the liberties of America than the whole force of the common enemy.... Neither the wisest constitution nor the wisest laws will secure the liberty and happiness of a people whose manners are universally corrupt."[30]

As long as the perpetrators of race grievance that are represented by the 1619 Project are permitted to go unchallenged, this country will continue its social, spiritual, and moral decline. 1776 Unites has enlisted a group of black scholars and social activists who uphold the true origins of our nation and the principles through which its founding promise can be fulfilled. While acknowledging that slavery and discrimination are part of our nation's history, we believe that America should not be defined solely by this "birth defect" and that black Americans should not be portrayed as perpetual helpless victims.

Rather than giving point-by-point counterarguments to the findings and conclusion of the 1619 Project, our focus will be to identify and highlight solutions, models of success in reviving our streets and communities, and actionable goals that should be pursued.

Key themes of 1776 Unites will be to:

Debunk the myth that present-day problems are related to our past, using evidence to confront the incomplete and misguided economic, historical, cultural, and religious positions taken by the 1619 Project—specifically, debunking the myth that slavery is the source of present-day disparities and injustice. America should not be defined by its failures.

Tell stories from the past and present of resilience and upward mobility. America should be defined by its promises.

We will tell the untold stories of people who have succeeded in the face of daunting obstacles, including slaves who became millionaires through entrepreneurial determination; former slaves who bought the plantations on which they once worked; present-day, inner-city grassroots leaders who are transforming drug-infested communities into peaceful, safe places to raise families; and others.

The stories of the successes of black Americans later will be complemented by examples of achievement against the odds by men, women, and youths representing a spectrum of races and ethnicities.

What America is confronting today, with the dominance of race grievance and identity politics, has had, since its inception, an even more sinister purpose: to maintain the political power of the landlord merchant class, according to historian James Oakes in his new book, *The Scorpion's Sting*. Oakes quotes Adolph L. Reed Jr., a political science professor at the University of Pennsylvania: "Identity is very much the ideology of the professional management class. They prefer to talk about identity over capitalism and the inequities of capitalism. We have an atrocious wealth gap in this country. It's not a black and white wealth gap. It's a wealth gap. But if you keep rephrasing it as black/white and shift it to a racial argument, you undermine the possibility of building a working-class coalition, which, by definition, would be disproportionately black, female, Latino, and still majority white. That's the kind of working-class coalition that identity politics tends to erase."[31]

Throughout her checkered past, America has been and remains a beacon of hope to people around the world. Join us in exploring stories of truth, perseverance, and triumph that acknowledge America's failures but celebrate her enduring promise.

THE ESSAYS

"A POSITIVE VISION: THE AGENDA OF '1776'"
BY WILFRED REILLY

The United States of American began in 1776, not 1619. I've found myself saying this quite a bit lately, in response to the claims of the *New York Times'* 1619 Project. The 1619 Project has argued, among other things, that the American Revolutionary War was fought to preserve slavery, that aggressive American capitalism is a legacy of slavery, and that historical racial segregation "caused your traffic jam."

Empirically, I believe that I and other members of the "1776" initiative—founder Robert L. Woodson Sr., Glenn Loury, Coleman Hughes, John Sibley Butler, Carol M. Swain, and Taleeb Starkes among them—have done a solid job of pointing out the weaknesses of the 1619 case and, more broadly, of the Howard Zinn-style radical social "science." To take just two of the points mentioned above: British colonies maintained the "peculiar institution" until fifty-two years after our revolution ended, and the most aggressively competitive economy in the world is generally Singapore's.[32]

But, there is another essay regarding 1776 to be written. When I speak or write about the initiative, easily the most common question I receive is: "But what do *you* guys believe?" The 1776 perspective can be condensed into one sentence: the U.S. is a flawed but very good country, where it is simply not terribly hard to succeed, given hard work and personal responsibility. As a founding member of 1776, I would personally draw this single thesis statement out into four points:

1. It is not accurate to claim that the contemporary U.S. is a "systemically" racist society;
2. Many of the primary social problems of today have nothing to do with historical racial conflict;
3. Individuals are not responsible for the sins of other members of their groups; and
4. Basic skills training—for example, test taking—would do far more to prep both blacks/minorities and working-poor white Americans for the real battles of today than would any amount of training in "grievance."

The first of these points is the most obviously accurate, but also the most controversial. The American activist Left argues constantly that the United States of 2020 is an "institutionally," "structurally," and "systemically" racist hell-state, chock-full of "white privilege" and "cultural appropriation(s)" and "microaggressions." In a widely cited 2018 essay, scholar Nicki Lisa Cole identified at least seven complicated forms of racism, including the "representative racism" of depicting blacks or Italians as criminals in films, the "discursive racism" of using such potentially loaded terms as "ghetto," and the "ideological racism" of believing in any ethnic stereotypes (for example, that Latin women tend to be fiery lovers and debaters) whatsoever.[33] Activist scholars frequently point to "prejudice" of this kind, in combination with legitimate historical atrocities such as lynching, to argue that people of color are systematically disadvantaged in the U.S.

The problem with this claim is that it is not true. No one disputes the bloody, unpleasant nature of large portions of American—and human—history. But, black and brown Americans have been on an even keel with the rest of our countrymen, at the level of literal federal law, for quite some time. The *Brown v. Board of Education* decision declared de jure racial segregation unconstitutional in 1954. The Civil

Rights Act went a big step further a decade later, making virtually all forms of racial discrimination civilly, and sometimes criminally, illegal. Even affirmative action is more than fifty years old, dating to President Nixon's Philadelphia Plan in 1967.

These legal protections are not merely words on paper, in the manner of the old Soviet Constitution. Affirmative action, in particular, provides a massive empirical advantage to virtually any non-Asian person of color applying for a Fortune 500 job or slot in a selective university. *The Harvard Crimson* recently noted that, among students admitted to Harvard, Asian Americans averaged a 767 score "across all sections" of the SAT exam; whites averaged 745; Hispanics, 718; and blacks, 704. All of these scores are quite solid, but their obvious implication is that a white student would have to score 82 more points than a black student, across just the math and verbal sections of the exam, to have the same chance at admission—and an Asian student would have to score 126 more points.[34] The affirmative action gap is even larger among students enrolled in good institutions one level down, sometimes ranging up to 300 points after the Ivies have poached the very best black and Hispanic students from the applicant pool.

In this context of relative equality or even situational minority advantage, a critical if rarely made point is that many common examples of "institutional racism" collapse when a basic adjustment for non-racial variables is made during a scholarly analysis. This fact has been an open secret among regression analysts and other "quants" for years. In 1995, government economist June O'Neill and conservative researcher Dinesh D'Souza both noted that the average black man earned only 82.9 percent of the white male wage, and that this disparity was often attributed to racism. However, adjusting for no variables but geographic/southern residency, age, years (not quality) of education, and aptitude test scores closed the gap to 4 percent. Tossing in years of work experience closed it to 1 percent. Similarly, the gap between white and black Americans in terms of the likelihood of being shot by the police—blacks make up 13 percent of the country and <u>25 to 30 percent of shooting victims</u> in a typical year—vanishes if an adjustment is made for the black crime rate, generally <u>2.1 to 2.4 times</u> the white rate.[35]

Further evidence for the non-nightmarish nature of contemporary America comes from the success of many recent minority immigrant groups. A 2014 Census Bureau graphic—so pleasantly surprising to many middle-class people of color that it became a trending online meme—noted that the highest-income racial/ethnic population in the United States is not WASPs, but rather Indian Americans, with a median household income of $100,295.[36] All told, eighteen groups finished ahead of whites, taken en bloc, including Taiwanese Americans ($85,500), Filipino Americans ($82,389), Lebanese Arabs ($69,586), and Nigerians ($61,289). American Jews, white or not, unsurprisingly also did well, with 44 percent of Jews living in households with incomes of $100,000 or more, and the Open Orthodox subcategory of Jews bringing home a remarkable $185,000 annually. There is no reason to believe that white racists fancy Yemini Jews or Yoruba tribesmen from Nigeria any more than black Americans, and the visible success of such groups illustrates that racism has declined dramatically—or, at the very least, that performance can dramatically overcome it.

A corollary to the fact that the U.S. is no longer a particularly racist or anti-Semitic country, in any historical or comparative sense, is the fact that many of today's problems in black or minority communities have little to do with present or past racism. This is often true to a rather surprising extent. Perhaps the best example of this trend is illegitimacy—or "out-of-wedlock birth," if you prefer. The black illegitimacy rate is currently 72 percent, and this is almost inevitably described as "a legacy of slavery." However, as right-leaning black economists such as Walter Williams have pointed out, the black illegitimacy rate was far lower when racism was much worse. In 1938, for example, only 11 percent of black children were born to unwed mothers. Almost unbelievably, under slavery, "one well-known 19th century study found that in three fourths of the families, all of the children had the same mother and father."

Perhaps the best evidence that modern family collapse is not because of anti-black racism is that it has not been confined entirely— or, in numerical terms, even primarily—to black people. In 2010, resources for homemakers such as *The Thinking Housewife* website began to note, with a notable lack of enthusiasm, that births to unmarried women had climbed above 40 percent of all American births for the first time. Such births were remarkably common among all races, making up 28.6 percent of the total for non-Hispanic whites (and 35 percent for all whites), 52.5 percent for Hispanics, and 72.3 percent for blacks. There is little, if any, doubt that out-of-wedlock birth rates for many regional and lower-income white groups currently stand well above 50 percent. Literally every large, non-Asian racial group in the United States "boasts" an out-of-wedlock birth rate well above the "shocking" 20-odd percent among blacks that triggered the famous Moynihan Report. This multi-colored problem is certainly disturbing, but literally impossible to blame on racism—and the same is true for many of the shared big issues of today.

A third "1776" point can be summed up as: even where past racism clearly did play a role in creating a problem we still see, as in the case of poverty housing, it is useless and indeed counterproductive to blame white Americans today for the sins of long-dead members of their ethnic group. All blacks are not responsible for black gang violence or crimes against whites, and all whites are not responsible for slavery. In the most obvious literal sense, a Caucasian individual whose ancestors were serfs in Sicily or Russia in 1864 had nothing to do with the peculiar institution, and basically the same holds true for the Jewish or Irish guy whose ancestors would have been trudging along shoeless in Union blue during the same year. Even a direct lineal descendant of Stonewall Jackson, one strongly suspects, might spend more time in 2020 taking his Italian American girlfriend to dinner and throwing passes to diverse buddies from the football team than secretly plotting the resurrection of the South. Accusing any of the individuals just described of nonsense such as "cultural appropriation" does nothing but fracture a potential problem-solving coalition of countrymen.

An especially awful effect of that fracturing is the almost universal neglect of poor whites, often dismissed as "deplorables," by the American taste-making class. Poor white Americans, almost by definition ineligible for both affirmative action and legacy programs, may be the most genuinely neglected population in the modern United States—making up the plurality or majority of those felled annually by suicide, auto wreck, and opiate and other drug overdoses. While less likely to catch the eye of the mainstream media that breathlessly reported urban homicides, these deaths of despair claim far more lives. In the fairly typical year of 2016, there were 17,250 recorded homicides in the United States, but 42,249 fatal drug overdoses, with 33,450 of those victims (79 percent) being non-Hispanic whites.

In this context, a very explicit goal of 1776 is "desegregating poverty." We plan to host an event in Appalachian Ohio headlined by Bob Woodson, columnist Clarence Page, and J. D. Vance, author of *Hillbilly Elegy*—that focuses on how Americans as a group can tackle the problems afflicting both poor black and poor white communities. In one of the entertaining ironies of our politically correct era, it just might take a group of well-off black guys to publicly stand up for poor white ones!

So, how *can* Americans as a group help struggling people tackle real problems? A solid, if hokey, two-word answer is "skills training." A point made earlier in this essay is that many of the performance gaps between groups that inevitably are attributed to institutional racism vanish once non-racial variables such as age and test scores are

8

adjusted for—and an obvious, if unspoken, fact is that non-Asian people of color and poor whites do very poorly against many of the tests used to measure success in modern societies. In 2017, the average SAT score was 1,181 for Asian Americans and 1,118 for whites as a group, but 941 for African Americans, 963 for Native Americans, and 987 for Hispanics. The disturbing alt-right tries to attribute these score gaps to genetics—a flawed theory for many reasons, notably including the fact that the Census Bureau classifies 50 to 75 percent of Hispanics as white—but the social scientists Fordham and Ogbu identified a simpler explanation in a magisterial late 1990s paper: minority kids study a lot less for the exam.

This may sound banal, but teaching study skills and other examples of what Amy Wax was pilloried for calling "bourgeois norms," as charter schools often do, will do far more to move working-poor Americans toward success than will teaching them African (or Celtic) meditation techniques and the Swahili word for "racism." Middle-class culture can be a bit pious and stifling, and it is occasionally fun to tweak the petit bourgeoisie. But this friendly cynicism is a luxury: one must learn how to be a successful adult, or at least play one in public, before testing the limits of that role. Preachers and rabbis have said from the pulpit for centuries that one has to do only three or four things in life to avoid poverty and failure: finish high school, take a job and work hard, wait until marriage to have children, avoid being convicted of a serious crime, and so forth. Empirical social science indicates this is very true—and this, rather than victimology, is the message to teach young people. "1776" is proud to have members such as Ian Rowe of Public Prep, who say exactly this on a daily basis.

The "1776" vision, at least as seen through my eyes, has four components:

1. Recognizing that the modern U.S. is a good society where people of all backgrounds can and often do succeed;

2. Rejection of racism as a catch-all explanation for black problems;

3. Advocating for alliances between blacks, whites, and others to solve American problems; and

4. Teaching useful skills, rather than basket-weaving "intersectional" nonsense.

"THE MORAL MEANING OF AMERICA: TWO PARALLEL NARRATIVES"
BY JASON D. HILL

Race has been endemic to American life from its inception. But I think race always was metaphysically irrelevant to the true spirit of America. Race, like the slavery that is America's tragic birth defect, was a betrayal of the essential moral meaning of America. When people come to America, past and present, they cannot adhere to their tribal lineage and ancestral past in any substantive way as a means of granting them a moral identity. Immigrants who arrive in America, while cosmetically hanging on to their tribal lineage, do not in any fundamental sense appeal to the traditions and customs of their old countries as ways of authenticating themselves over time. One lives not by appeal to ancestry, but by acts used to ratify the validity and legitimacy of one's personal existence.

Americans are the first individualists and, by design, the first non-tribal people in the world.

We may say that the one state in human history that has inserted itself into the world and the global imagination, and offered itself up as a home, a refuge,[37] a place where any person can be welcomed and offered a chance to fulfill any aspiration and goal, was and remains the United States. Today, there are other countries, of course, that fulfill this goal, including Canada, France, and Great Britain. Yet, because

America was founded as a nation of immigrants—a cosmopolitan melting pot—it not only has provided the cosmopolitan with an existential referent, a home, but also has reversed a trend in political life that has marked human societies since recorded history. It has undermined the degree of tribalism at the heart of citizenship—belonging—and the notion of community by making all such distinctions not just irrelevant, but ethically untenable.

The United States has transformed the moral and political prism through which we see and evaluate the status of the aspiring citizen by fundamentally changing the way we formulate the moral qualifications and credentials a person must have to become a citizen of the republic. The answer is, of course, nothing but their naked, singular humanity, with certain rational qualifiers that have nothing to do with tribal affiliation.

Inserted as a nontribal unprecedented phenomenon in the world, the United States has achieved a unique feat of political eugenics. Instead of being an imitator, it is a model for emulation.[38] America has detribalized the world by offering up its model as worthy of universal emulation; it has functioned as an ethical domain in which resocialization of a certain type takes place.

By making foreigners and strangers into Americans, the republic has made them citizens of the world by undermining and de-ratifying the spirit of seriousness grafted onto lineage and blood identity. The American by birth or, even more so, by naturalization is the concretization of a world citizen, because what is central to belonging and citizenship are moral purpose (the inviolable freedom to create one's own conception of the good life for oneself) and a moral-political commitment to adhere to the fundamental defining principles of the republic grounded, as it were, in a philosophy of individualism.

Explicit adherence to a philosophy of individualism provides the litmus test for how and when one's actions can be exercised in the world against the freedoms and rights of another. Individualism and its political corollary in the form of individual rights subordinate society to political laws derived from moral laws. This commitment to the principles defending individualism and individual rights, in a robustly political sense, gave birth to the rise of the individual and enacted what the honorable ancient Stoics[39] could only have dreamed of: the creation of a republican polity that could be home to all citizens of the world by formal principle.

America is the first country to insert itself into the world and offer itself up as a friend to humanity; it's the place where citizens from anywhere can belong and play a role in suffusing the nation-state with an original assemblage of who one is.

The United States is the first full-fledged cosmopolitan state for all the reasons advanced previously and more: America encourages human beings not to search for their origins, but, rather, their destiny. It is the first nation in human history where—in spite of lip service to hyphenated identities that are purely symbolic—human beings have been driven to flee their origins and remake themselves through a process of becoming a new specimen, often a radically new man or woman.

Identity makeovers are fully possible only in the United States of America. The social reality that thoroughly suffused an "Untouchable's" life in India has no existential counterpart in the United States, a country where most Americans are properly unconcerned with the term and the nefarious caste system it denotes. The "Untouchable" lands in America and is perceived as South Asian and, more or less, nothing more than that. Her socioeconomic mobility in America, her associations, and her right to forget where she came from are within her powers. Whereas, in her native India, she was stamped with the mark of closure and social completeness, America grants her the freedom not just to become, but to wipe her social slate clean in order to become, in order to realize her not-as-yet-self. America grants her a philosophy of life that is itself a disclosure of possibilities.

America was the first country that incentivized the individual to prioritize the future over the past, to eschew nostalgia in favor of hope and aspiration.

We are a reformed society. No other country has ever included within the domain of the ethical such units of moral concern during so short a time in its nascent existence as the many persons and groups have in America. Nearly 244 years after its creation, there are no persons or individuals who, on principle, can be excluded from the domain of the ethical and of justice.

There have been, and shall continue to be, concrete examples of individuals who have been excluded; however, it is safe to say that part of the moral meaning of the United States lies in its ever-widening pantheon of inclusiveness. America is the first immigrant country in history predicated on civic nationalism—which includes the membership principle but transcends it in that persons beyond its shores, such as immigrants, refugees, stateless peoples, and other victims of political and economic oppression, are both welcomed and invited into the United States to seek more than just ameliorative and reparative status in the republic.

This is America, where a third founding (taking Lincoln's promise at Gettysburg and the Civil War as the second) was achieved in the civil rights movement and the passage of the 1964 Civil Rights Act. The inclusive promise of "We the People" was finally delivered to all people in this country. The formal debt owed to black people for centuries of enslavement and inexcusable mistreatment and exclusion from mainstream American society was paid.

America has always been a place of regeneration, renewal, and self-examination, a place where peoplehood is not a given or a smug achievement, but, rather, a long and continuous aspiration.

There is a reason that "Matilda," the maid from Africa or Mexico or Jamaica, oppressed as she might feel by a dominant class structure in her native country, can flee the hermetically sealed nature of those systems and come to America. There is a reason that boatloads of peasants from Haiti and Cuba and other countries have risked their lives in makeshift rafts and leaky boats to seek hope and a better way of life here in America. These people are largely black people. America gives all of them a space to negotiate its ongoing moral narrative.

America works!

We must not forget that it was in America in 1903 at Ellis Island that immigrants arriving to this magnificent nation were greeted by a copper statue, the Statue of Liberty, whose pedestal bears the words of Emma Lazarus: "Give me your tired, your poor, your huddled masses yearning to breathe free, the wretched refuse of your teeming shore. Send these the homeless, tempest-tossed to me. I lift my lamp beside the golden door."[40]

The essence of that invitation came in a clarion call for people of all types to be reborn into a new type of man or woman: the new American.

This gift-giving feature of our humanity—anathema to the spirit of every variant of tribalism, whether it takes the form of cultural nationalism or racial particularity—is the humble capacity to genuflect before the "other" in a spirit of reciprocity, in respectful brotherhood and sisterhood, and say: I am not so complete that I can resist handing over to you some part of my continued socialization and identity formation as a human being. With you, my friend, my humanity, regardless of its origins, continues to expand and will take me to places I could never have imagined.

I have fallen quite a few times in my journey through the American landscape as I traverse the paths towards my goals. I have picked myself up and looked towards the frontier.

Not once has America disappointed me.

"ACKNOWLEDGING SLAVERY'S LIMITS IN DEFINING AMERICA"
BY JOHN WOOD JR.

To be black in America is to have some relationship to the historic tragedy of slavery. American slavery, often referred to as a type of chattel slavery, was unique as a condition of servitude in the tortured history of forced bondage in the human race. Whereas, before the trans-Atlantic slave trade, the institution of slavery as it existed across continents and time periods typically allowed forced servitude to exist as a consequence of military defeat or financial debt, chattel slavery in the Americas relied on the active capturing or purchasing of Africans whose continued enshacklement was justified (in the racial ideology that evolved) as the proper expression of the natural hierarchy of the races.

From such insidious origins, the evolution of many American institutions, and much in the way of the education and psychological formation of black Americans themselves, was affected. Yet in recognizing this fact, black Americans—and all Americans today—should also recognize that it is possible that the effect of slavery and racial oppression on our society today grows largely out of the power that we choose to give it. Slavery is limited in its ability to determine the success of black Americans in our present day. The legacy of slavery is not what determines the fundamental character of our country— unless we choose for that to be so.

In the spring of 2008, on the verge of winning the Democratic nomination for president, Barack Obama delivered a landmark address on the subject of race to a nation still somewhat dubious about the prospect of a black man becoming president of the United States. Obama opened by making a quick reference to "this nation's original sin of slavery," noting that it left "unfinished"[41] the liberating work of the Declaration of Independence.

Yet he proceeded to observe that in the ideals that informed America's Founding were sown the seeds of its redemption: "Of course, the answer to the slavery question was already embedded within our Constitution—a Constitution that had at its very core the ideal of equal citizenship under the law; a Constitution that promised its people liberty and justice and a union that could be and should be perfected over time.

"And yet words on a parchment would not be enough to deliver slaves from bondage, or provide men and women of every color and creed their full rights and obligations as citizens of the United States," he continued. "What would be needed were Americans in successive generations who were willing to do their part...to narrow that gap between the promise of our ideals and the reality of their time."[42]

That is true. And this truth provides the understandable root of a claim by Nikole Hannah-Jones, chief editor for the *New York Times*' 1619 Project, that "Our democracy's founding ideals were false when they were written. Black Americans have fought to make them true."[43]

Indeed, black Americans, alongside many others, have fought for generations to deliver America to her higher values. But there is something linguistically confused about suggesting American ideals (or anyone's ideals, for that matter) are false. Ideals are not statements of fact to be true or false; they are just that: ideals. They are the better realities to which we aspire. Thus, the narrative of many individuals who believe the United States ought to be defined more by her moral failings than by her moral triumphs and aspirations tends to be one that de-emphasizes our nation's proven ability to overcome these moral failings. The heart of American history is diminished in so doing.

There are sympathetic reasons for this way of seeing America, however, particularly when it comes to the moral failing of slavery. In his epic essay for *The Atlantic*, "The Case for Reparations," Ta-Nehisi Coates asserts that the great thrust of black history in America threatens America's ability to look at itself the way that it wants to. Thus, the idea of reparations exposes us to a conversation in which the white majority and those of us invested in an idealistic understanding of the nation's history stand unprepared to engage—that is, a conversation about the immoral magnitude of the transgressions that stain America's past and present vis-à-vis its treatment of black people. The threat of reparations to such idealistic Americans is about more than money: "The idea of reparations threatens something much deeper—America's heritage, history, and standing in the world."[44]

According to Coates, "Black history does not flatter American democracy; it chastens it. The popular mocking of reparations as a harebrained scheme authored by wild-eyed lefties and intellectually unserious black nationalists is fear masquerading as laughter."[45]

Coates may be right. There is a depth of anguish and a long story of both crude and sophisticated persecution of black Americans that originates with slavery but runs through the story of black American history in nearly every major region and time period. One never even needs to study the antebellum South and Jim Crow laws to be appalled by the racial history of New York City, Los Angeles, or Chicago. Yet, until recently, relatively few Americans were familiar with the history of redlining; the ghettoization of black communities through New Deal housing policies[46]; the cruelty in the historic practice of medicine involving black Americans[47]; and all of the ways in which these historical injustices can be traced back to slavery, and forward to a current moment that, in various ways, still echoes with the consequences.

Because these things happened, and do indeed have consequences, our understanding of America must take them into account.

Writers such as Coates and the contributors to the 1619 Project do a thorough job of reacquainting us with uncomfortable streams of our history, which in places run more like rivers. They recall facts that some may prefer to ignore, but which ought not be forgotten.

But to make limitless the effect of slavery and historical racism on the current moment is to risk overlooking the ways in which black Americans have overcome these and other obstacles by holding to the values that informed the nation's founding, and that have been traditionally recognized as the virtues by which American society has achieved preeminence: a stalwart defense of liberty and equality as ideals to which all human beings are rightfully entitled, and an embrace of faith, family, and communal solidarity that has made black culture in America arguably its most enduring and distinctive (the relative deterioration of which in the aftermath of the Great Society[48] is arguably the most salient threat facing black America).

As Nikole Hannah-Jones would seem to suggest, black Americans have epitomized these foundational values. But in so doing, black history does not belie them as definitively American ideals—it confirms them. So, too, does the long history of white Americans and others who took up arms and pens in defense of these rights and virtues alongside the black community.

In diminishing the idea that racism in American history and its lingering effects are overcome by the enterprise, family grounding, and moral courage of Americans (and those who emigrate to this country in search of the American Dream), one also risks gliding by the wide body of evidence demonstrating that people of exactly similar ethnic appearance (including black people) in America have succeeded at wildly different rates. They have outperformed other groups, depending on the cultural disposition they bring to life in the United States. My fellow contributor to 1776 Unites, Coleman Hughes, has done an admirable job highlighting this fact by comparing the educational and economic outcomes of immigrants from the West Indies to native-born black Americans in his *Quillette* essay, "The Racism Treadmill."[49]

But even culture itself evolves according to history, Coates argues. If there are flaws in black American culture that account for some of today's problems, they exist as a byproduct of an American history that begins with slavery, continuing in an unending epoch of racism. Fair enough—a people's history cannot be disconnected from its culture. But what we choose to emphasize in our history reflects in our culture, and in the stories we tell ourselves that determine how we relate to this country and what is possible for us within it.

In his introduction to *The Classic Slave Narratives,* historian Henry Louis Gates makes a compelling observation about slaves in the United States: "One of the most curious aspects of the African person's enslavement in the New World is that he and she wrote about the severe conditions of their bondage."

He continues: "In the long history of human bondage, it was only the black slaves in the United States who...created a genre of literature that at once testified against their captors and bore witness to the urge of every black slave to be free and literate. Hundreds of ex-slaves felt compelled to tell their tales on the anti-slavery lecture circuit in the North and in the written form of the autobiographical narrative."[50]

Who has the greater claim to the legacy of America—the men who enslaved their fellow human beings in contradiction of the principles that guided the nation's founding, or the slaves who, through a greater belief in freedom, added to the canon of freedom that enriches America's understanding of herself to this day? Who has the greater claim—those white people who defended the "peculiar institution" or those white people who enthusiastically received Frederick Douglass and Harriet Jacobs on the lecture circuit, plus the thousands upon thousands who read their books and pushed forward the cause of freedom? Do the triumphs of these devotees to freedom and equality in

America begin a story about our nation's moral failures, or is it a story about America's long march toward her higher aspirations?

The answer to this question depends on what we, as Americans, choose to define our nation and ourselves by. This, in turn, will determine what our nation will become.

"WE CANNOT ALLOW '1619' TO DUMB DOWN AMERICA IN THE NAME OF A CRUSADE"
BY JOHN MCWHORTER

The data are in: the *New York Times*' 1619 Project[51] is founded on empirical sand. The fundamental claim that the Revolutionary War was fought to preserve slavery simply does not correspond with the facts, too conclusively for the point to be dismissed as mere hair-splitting. The issue is not differing interpretations of history, but an outright misinterpretation of it.

Yet the project lives on. Its spearheaders blithely dismiss the charges of inaccuracy as mere natterings that at least verge on racism, while school districts nationwide eagerly receive pedagogical materials based on the idea of offering students a fresh, revealing take on American history.

We must ask: Is there some broader aspect of the 1619 Project that justifies a certain slippage between its claims and actual fact? Just what does this project have to teach students? What does it have to teach us? And if the answer to those questions is "nothing much," then how is it that brilliant, high-placed people can be so serenely unruffled in promulgating this material to innocent young minds?

In the end, the 1619 Project is more than a history lesson. It is founded on three basic principles, none expounded with a great deal of clarity, but all of them pernicious to a truly constructive black American identity.

One takeaway from the *Times'* rhetoric is that the American experiment offers nothing to celebrate, definitionally polluted by its dependence for so long on unpaid labor by black people. Our red-blooded celebration of 1776 as a political and even moral and intellectual victory is, under this analysis, callow and backward. In their minds, 1776 was a culmination of a grisly beginning 157 years before, of a kind no one could dream of feting with fireworks and barbecues.

For all of its emotional resonance, this assertion is so simplistic and anti-intellectual that both rationality and morality require dismissing it. For example, one corollary of this viewpoint is a discomfort with seeing America's Founding Fathers honored as heroes and pioneers. We are taught that, because these men either owned slaves or let pass that others did, we are to see them as morally repugnant. In a recent radio interview, a black journalist discussed a book she has written documenting the racist aspects of all of the U.S. presidents. She argued that we must be "honest" about these figures instead of settling for a sanitized vision of what these men did and tolerated. The host, a black woman, very civilly asked her for what purpose we should keep these things about these men in mind.

The historian only repeated her point about "honesty" a few times; she seemed a tad thrown by the angle of the question. One sensed that she was refraining from saying directly that we are not to think of George Washington, John Adams, Thomas Jefferson, Abraham Lincoln, or even Franklin D. Roosevelt as heroes, that musicals such as *1776*, films such as *Lincoln*, and the endless stream of august biographies celebrating such men are inappropriate. The protean musical

Hamilton actually has been critiqued in this vein for not holding front and center that slaves were keeping the New York he knew afloat, and that Alexander Hamilton was not sufficiently committed to arguing against slavery.

This way of thinking calls for pretty much any white figure before now to wear scarlet letters on their heads. The letter today presumably would be R for "racist." Everyone knew Nathaniel Hawthorne's Hester Prynne was a kind person in many ways, but Hawthorne portrayed a society whose morality decreed that her adultery be treated as a defining trait, relegating all else about her to triviality. Almost all of us, including many very religious people, today look upon this as benighted; the book is used in schools as an object lesson in how censorious obsessions of the moment can lead to unthinking cruelty. However, the 1619 Project puts forth that this kind of moral absolutism is correct in the case of American slavery.

That slavery was almost universally condoned at the time, an ordinary feature of life that one grew up immersed in unquestioned, and at a time when much less was known about science or the wider world, is considered irrelevant. We are to think of the sin of slavery as overriding all considerations of context, of what it is to be a human being, of, in a word, complexity.

Here, then, is the problem: The 1619 kind of perspective, for all of its elaborate terminology and moral passion vented in serious media organs and entertained by people with PhDs, demands that we abjure complexity. It is a call for dumbing ourselves down in the name of a moral crusade.

America has always been an experiment, ever imperfect, always in rehearsal. That its beginnings four hundred years ago were founded in casual bondage of other humans is appalling from our viewpoint but should surprise no one given what was ordinary in all human societies worldwide at the time. That, in this nation, slavery gradually was abolished, via a movement in which white people vigorously and crucially participated, was a kind of miracle in itself. It demonstrated that the rehearsal was a progressive one, moving ever towards justice even if never achieving its quintessence.

The 1619 adherent rolls their eyes to hear that, as if some larger and obvious point is being missed. However, they have failed to communicate any such point that stands up to basic scrutiny, and meanwhile, it is they who miss a larger point: what social history actually is. Frankly, the 1619 vision, in pretending that the roiling, complex history of the United States can be reduced to the fate of one group of people within it, abused, oppressed, and dismissed though they were for so very long, is lazy. Constitutional history matters only in that slaves were counted as three-fifths of a person. Feminism matters only in that white feminists were racists by our standards. Economic history matters only in relation to the yield from plantations. Geopolitics matters only in terms of whether the British would have abolished slavery in America. Technology matters only in terms of the cotton gin.

The entire business absolves one of the responsibility to engage the vast spectrum of human affairs that history constitutes, with the methods of inquiry and engagement long established as its modus operandi. To engage history openly and thoroughly becomes almost disloyal, inauthentic. History itself does not interest these people as much as something more local, personal even.

Thought experiment: Imagine the 1619 crowd's response to a version of American history stressing the fate of white women, asserting that the patriarchy always has and continues to deny women's humanity and that this is the guiding force of American history, having made the rise of the republic possible. Immediately, our 1619-ers would grasp that as grievous as the history of women in America (and worldwide) is, a vision of this kind is reductive, appealing largely to a small group most would see as highly ideological.

Yet the 1619 idea is similar. Slavery was hideous in endless ways, but it was still, in the grand scheme of things—and there was one—

just one of a great many things going on. And if all of those things can be cleverly traced to the black people toiling in fields, sheds, and pantries, then so too can they be traced to the women often doing similar things and undergoing different kinds of abuse, including what women historians today convincingly limn as denials of their humanity.

And never mind how often people of the 1619 mindset get even their history wrong. Their guiding idea is that to closely engage all of this "white" history, and certainly to see anything in it to praise, is as if one were doing all of this while a slave was being whipped just beyond the corner of one's eye.

Abraham Lincoln's Emancipation Proclamation doesn't matter because he also for a while thought slaves, once freed, should be transported back to Africa. Lyndon Johnson's Great Society must be remembered as the product of a man who gleefully referred to "niggers" in private and made nice with open segregationists. Black women who love Hillary Clinton must ever recall that she once referred to certain black gang members as "superpredators."[52]

We are to keep ever at the forefront of our minds that all of these blights and torts are the spawn of something so conclusively revolting that it eliminates any reason to seriously consider anything else about these people in evaluating them as human figures or, by extension, America as an accomplishment. America's very foundation, the heart of what America has ever been, is a denial of black people's humanity. As such, we must conceive of all of these white big names with big Rs on their foreheads—and of course, all modern whites must wear big Ps for "privilege" on theirs.

A smart ten-year-old could see through the willful cluelessness on which this supposedly enlightened conception of social history is based. Who seriously condemns persons of the past for being unable to see beyond the confines of their time, when the ability to do this is precisely what we otherwise consider one of the quintessences of greatness? Or to anticipate a likely objection, who thinks the ability to see beyond the confines of one's time is the very definition of greatness, such that we must disqualify the Founding Fathers because despite whatever else they did that might seem to court greatness, they could not see beyond their time enough to grasp the full humanity of black people and therefore fell conclusively short?

The illogic here is plain to anyone. Only a certain etiquette today makes enough non-blacks refrain from acknowledging that the types who promulgate tropes such as the 1619 Project are able to do so with so little self-questioning and such impatience with critique. This is a way of looking at the past familiar from Marxist ideology, training adherents Zen-style to carefully stanch reasonable disbelief in favor of slogans, to tamp down a desire to explore, discover, and reason with a commitment to broad-stroked evangelism. If the 1619 Project has a defensible justification, this perspective on history is not one of them.

Or, suppose it is? One might understand that 1619-style history is propaganda masquerading as thought, while supposing that to wink and let it pass is worthwhile in view of a larger agenda. Take the evangelism I referred to above—is the 1619 perspective geared towards achieving a result beyond the historiographical that will uplift black America in such a way that we might hearken to John Ford's call to "print the legend" when it serves a worthy purpose?

One purpose the 1619 idea could serve is to reanimate the idea that black Americans are owed reparations for the salary denied their slave ancestors. Nikole Hannah-Jones has stated[53] that this is the ultimate goal of the proposal she has been central in spearheading, for example.

However, we must ask why Hannah-Jones has only stated this in an almost parenthetical fashion. If the point is intended to get black people reparational payments, then we would expect that this would have been headlined front and center, rather than the idea being largely presented as a mere history lesson.

A charitable explanation for why the reparations aim has been backgrounded so by 1619 proponents is a sense among them that the reparations argument is so poorly received in so many quarters—including many black ones—that it is most effectively presented in a backdoor manner. After all, the initial national discussion of the idea in the 1970s went nowhere, and its revival in the late 1990s also was longer on heat than result, leaving Congressman John Conyers Jr. quietly entering his reparations bill year after year in what became a kind of quiet gesture of protest rather than a plan of action. While Ta-Nehisi Coates's noteworthy article[54] reignited the idea, after all of the attention paid, it would be hard to say that the idea has gotten any further beyond the stirring but empty symbolism of the 2020 Democratic presidential candidates paying lip service to it in line with current "woke" expectations.

Possibly, then, reparations are best put over via stealth, in the way that an evangelist might try to bring someone into their fold by first asking their interlocutor whether they sense a lack of direction in their lives, whether they believe in something larger, and so on. Here, we learn that the American experiment actually begins with black people brought to these shores in bondage (actually, they apparently were indentured servants, not slaves). So generations of black people after this worked without pay under brutal conditions, and then after emancipation, their descendants were treated little better, in many quarters until as late as the 1960s. It might seem to naturally follow that modern black people are owed some money.

Note, however, that the last sentence above feels a touch hasty to most readers beyond those already converted to the idea of reparations. The entire argument always has been a fragile one in countless dimensions, with this having as much to do with the resistance to it as racism and indifference. For one, the very notion that today's problems in black America trace to what happened in 1619 is more a Rube Goldberg-style mental stunt than actual social history, vastly oversimplifying a much more complex, and in many ways more heartening, story; Coleman Hughes has outlined this quite usefully.[55]

Then, Yale University law professor Boris Bittker's book on reparations,[56] now forty-eight years old, politely but comprehensively fileted the whole idea so conclusively that it continues to stand as the last word on the matter. Those under the impression that Coates's article in the *Atlantic* has superseded it would feel otherwise if they read Bittker's book—unless they operate under the indefensible conceit that a book on reparations is logically and morally valid only if written by someone black. Both Coates's article and Randall Robinson's *The Debt*[57] of 2000, as eagerly and widely discussed just twenty years ago as Coates's article has been, are largely eloquent cris de coeur in the place of pragmatic analysis. Coates brings in some information about redlining; Robinson was more concerned with Africa. Both, however, largely punt on specifics.

In general, then, if the 1619 idea is an indirect way of calling for reparations for slavery, there are two problems. One is that this call has failed to bear real fruit for longer than most black people now have been alive. It renders the 1619 proposal old wine in what is now a battered and half-empty bottle. Second is that the proponents of the 1619 idea apparently lack the confidence in their reparational aims to even present them directly—or at best, are under an impression that hints, implications, and parentheticals can be an effective way of swaying a vast and diverse populace regarding a radical, controversial proposal. This is not only old wine in an old bottle, but to borrow another alcohol-related metaphor that Sen. Amy Klobuchar (D-Minn.) used in reference to something else during the Democratic debates of summer 2019, this is "all foam and no beer."[58]

The 1619 analysis is also designed to serve as an explanation for disparities between black and white achievement. The lesson, sometimes openly stated, is that all such deficits trace to the disadvantage that black people were saddled with by being brought to America in chains. This grows from a basic tenet among perhaps most black academics in the humanities and social sciences, as well as other black people of the "woke" mindset. That tenet is that America must understand that there is "nothing wrong with" black people. These people fairly ache to see Americans master the mental trick, the moral generosity, to look upon black-white disparities and understand that the reason for these is black people's lack of "agency," as sociologists put it. We must understand that tomatoes are fruits, that gravity means that people in the Southern Hemisphere do not fall off the earth, that mountains wear down to create sand—and that black problems are "not our fault."

And to be sure, in terms of how these disparities began, they are not "our fault." If black people had come to America on their own steam, and somehow not been processed by whites here as animals, we can be quite sure there would not be the disproportion of black people in urban inner-city neighborhoods, the subpar scholastic achievement (if anyone doubts that, consult studies that documented sky-high IQs among plenty of black students in Chicago in the 1930s), and so much else. The pathway from 1619 to 2020 is vastly more tortuous than we are being taught to believe—that is, today we would not find that kind of IQ performance among those very students' great-grandchildren, for reasons that trace to "racism" only in ways the 1619 crowd would find inconvenient; consult Stuart Buck's *Acting White: The Ironic Legacy of Desegregation.*[59] However, in the grand scheme of things, it is indeed not "our fault."

Too seldom asked, however, is why it is so important what white people think of us. To precisely what end must white people master a complex, nuanced social history lesson when it comes to black people? What are the chances that this ever will, or even could, happen, given that very few people are historians or professors? Of course, we must battle the kind of acrid contempt that leads to violence and murder. However, when it comes to matters of whites' quieter dismissive attitudes and misimpressions, the black intelligentsia's Ahab-like commitment to transforming their mentality has always perplexed me. Under what conception of human strength do we teach a group of people to obsess over how they are seen in the eyes of others?

More specifically, how is this Black Power? The idea seems to be that for black people—and only us—it is a kind of human strength to obsess with Talmudic intensity over whether white people like us, value us, truly see us equals, and in just which ways. For black people, the cry of powerlessness is somehow a form of strength, and even racial authenticity. However, actual defenses of that idea seem not to exist. The detractor objects that no one has said that whites' attitudes were so important—but the fact that the 1619 Project is founded upon exactly such a concern neatly deep-sixes this objection. And the fact remains that this obsession with white people understanding that it "isn't our fault" goes against the basics of what we consider healthy tutelage to any human being. "Who cares what he thinks about you?" we tell our child. The psychologist treats minimization of obstacles, an almost willful denial, as a healthy kind of coping strategy for busy humans grappling with the challenges of life.

But our wise ones tell us that when it comes to black people, things are different. Authentic blackness means refraining from any natural inclination to minimization. Our entire self-conception as a race is supposed to be founded on the fact that whites see us as inferior, upon a wariness of how whites feel about us, and even a sense of fellowship as people communally "oppressed" by the fact that whites don't quite see us with the dignity and precision we would prefer.

My intent here is not to encourage the reader to simply dismiss people such as the 1619 advocates as "crazy." We must attempt to get at the heart of what these intelligent, morally concerned people suppose. Here, it is reasonable to surmise that they think this focus on whether it's "our fault" has some kind of benefit that makes it worth it to battle minimization, that makes it somehow advanced, progressive, to obsess over obstacles, rather than seek to get around them.

For example, one might suppose that if more people understood that "it isn't our fault," then societal changes that would elevate black America would happen faster. That vision is easy to accommodate from a distant, vague perspective. However, we must ask: What is the evidence that this is true? In what other human society did the ruling class's understanding that "it isn't their fault" condition a change in an oppressed group's fortunes? Note that the only real example is this very society, where exactly this happened with black people during the civil rights revolution of the 1950s and 1960s. It seems that today's warriors suppose that further, deeper understanding of this kind could fashion even more change.

However, the simple question is: Who are the people who, if they underwent a grand realization that "it isn't their fault" beyond the basic "root causes" wisdom, now entrenched among the educated for fifty years, would fashion impactful changes in legislation on health, drugs, education, or housing? Which officials, in which positions? What exactly are we thinking they would do? "I finally understood that the problems in black communities trace back to injustices that began in the seventeenth century, and that is what finally made me _____." With what would the 1619 people fill in that blank?

A common riposte here will be that what makes the "it's not their fault" argument especially important is that the black experience is defined by experiencing racism not just as a passing attitude but in the form of violence at the hands of the police. We will leave aside that the universality of this experience among black people is vastly exaggerated—as Ellis Cose, likely in favor of the 1619 position, has stated, "Most middle-class blacks know that they are not very likely to find themselves on the wrong side of a policeman's baton."[60]

However, in general, after the room is done clapping and amening and snapping their fingers, to bring the cops into this is more something someone would think of as a defense than an actual argument. Via what strategy are we hoping to teach the typical cop the lesson "it isn't their fault," and most importantly, how would that relate to whether or not they hurt or killed a black person in the heat of the moment? The 1619 advocate is caught in a bind here, dedicated to pointing out how ineradicably racism is imprinted in the white soul while also preparing to claim that some articles in the *New York Times Magazine* are going to transform that white soul's psyche.

Countless human groups have succeeded amidst dismissive attitudes, and in societies in which no one cared the slightest about the intricacies of how social history held them back. The modern black intelligentsia's claim is that for some reason, in the late twentieth century in the United States there emerged a situation in which one particular oppressed class, the descendants of African slaves, could only fitfully succeed once the ruling class underwent a profound transformation not just in how it ran things, but in how it thought, down all the way to its basal, precortical impulses.

Gone are the days when a true civil rights leader such as Bayard Rustin could, in his renowned *Commentary* article[61] in 1965, carefully outline just how black people could succeed despite the challenges of automation and what the ruling culture would need to provide, in the concrete rather than psychological sense, to allow this to be so. Nowhere are we taught why today's psychological focus is a preferable approach, rather than a mere fashion. And perplexingly, nowhere in these people's writings and talks do we see any hint of the shame that you would expect someone to feel in lustily proclaiming their own people as uniquely incapable of coping with a challenging reality.

To the extent that answers to the questions raised here either dance around or dismiss them, we understand that the entire 1619 edifice is founded on something other than pragmatism.

To accept the implication of the 1619 ideology that heroic figures should be dismissed for not fully understanding the horrors of slavery, and that the American story is defined by nothing except the treatment of black people, would be to disrespect them as infantile minds. As such, we must evaluate the project on what it portends for forging socio-political change. Sadly, here the project would seem to yield nothing. A revivification of the reparations argument is longer on theatre than politics. The concern with whites understanding that "it isn't our fault" may seem a form of political engagement but in fact is quite irrelevant to change in actual lives.

Rather, the 1619 message is, alone, the action in itself. To many black thinkers today, they sense that the Cassandra role is what makes black thought most interesting. It also makes a black thinker feel important, like they matter. There is an insecurity being assuaged here, an understandable product of a race subjected to such dismissal for centuries. Black America is still working that out, despite the new freedoms afforded us fifty years ago, and among the black intelligentsia, this also explains the hypersensitivity about whether whites "understand." That kind of hypersensitivity is a product of self-doubt. A people who truly like themselves don't give a damn whether other people like them and take pride in the very act of succeeding regardless.

But what this means is that, evaluated honestly, the 1619 Project is a kind of performance art. Facts, therefore, are less important than attitude. Hannah-Jones has predictably dismissed serious and comprehensive empirical critiques, as if for black thinkers, truth is somehow ranked second to fierceness and battle poses. For many, questioning the 1619 Project elicits irritation, of a kind that suggests personal insult rather than difference of opinion. This is because the 1619 Project is indeed all about personality, a certain persona that smart black people are encouraged to adopt as a modern version of being a civil rights warrior.

For this 2.0 version of a civil rights warrior, authentic blackness, significant blackness, requires eternal opposition, bitter indignation, and claims of being owed. Whether all of this is rooted in reality in a way that can create change for actual human beings is of less concern than whether all of this is expressed, on a regular basis. It keeps The Struggle going, we are told.

How sad that the wandering socio-historical trajectory that got us from 1619 to here can create a caste among the oppressed who, in all sincerity, mistake performance for activism. If we really want to get anywhere, the tragedy is that today we must take a deep breath and forge a new Struggle against them and their influence. Ironically, we must understand, despite the performers' tongue-clucking and nasty tweets and GIFs, that it will be those engaged in this new Struggle who will qualify, in a truly proactive sense, as authentically black.

"SLAVERY DOES NOT DEFINE THE BLACK AMERICAN EXPERIENCE"
BY WILFRED REILLY

S lavery was horrible, but it was not the primary factor that built this country, and its historical existence does not permanently stain our nation's legacy. It should never be denied—and no one in fact does deny this—that the "land of the free" once used captives from other societies almost as cattle. However, the reality is that virtually all societies existing before the modern era did so, and only one became the United States of America. Logically, something other than our past indulgence of evil must be responsible for our current greatness.

Slavery in the United States existed, by definition, only from our actual national founding in 1776 until the end of the Civil War in 1865, and existed almost entirely in the agrarian South[62] during that period. There is essentially no evidence that the practice boosted the wealth of that region beyond that of the rest of the U.S.: the South was widely considered a feudal backwater even before the Union army conquered it, killing roughly one in four military-aged males in the region during the process. Virtually all American industrial and economic development has taken place since that occurred.

Further, and importantly, slavery does not empirically seem to be the cause of most modern problems even in the black community.

Remarkably, the black illegitimacy rate[63] was far lower under slavery than it is today.

Every point just made matters and is worth hashing out. First, almost literally no one denies that slavery was bad. American bondage was a fairly harsh form of chattel slavery, a system within which individuals are deprived of personal liberty and forced to submit to an owner—who can buy, lease, or sell them like any other form of property. The writings of the ancient Greeks, who knew this system well, describe (often unintentionally) its dehumanizing brutality. The writer Xenophon recommends[64] treating slaves like intelligent domestic animals, while great Aristotle himself describes the life of a slave as being composed of "work, beatings," and, if the poor fellow was lucky, "feedings." American slave masters seem to have been no better than Greek ones: to read through slave narratives is to be deluged with stories of coarse and scanty food, brutal whip-wielding overseers, runaways chased down by dogs, and young children "sold down the river." Portions of American, and human, history are written in blood, and can be difficult for modern eyes to read.

But, with all that said and unexcused—this essay will not dwell on the significantly greater prevalence of slavery in Latin America, or the Muslim states of the Middle East, than in the United States—the plain fact is that the U.S. did not begin in 1619, and even the slavery that existed in 1776 had a fairly limited impact on who we are as a society today. In 1619, the year in which the *New York Times* recently declared[65] America actually began, there were an estimated 210 English-speaking settlers on the North American continent, perhaps 20 of whom were black slaves. Even by the time of the first national census in 1790, more than a decade after independence, there were roughly 3.9 million Americans. Only 19.3 percent[66] of these people were of African descent, and by no means were all of the blacks slaves. More than a few, in fact, were slave owners.

As early as that same year, slaveholders of whatever race would have found their "peculiar institution" welcome in less than half of the country. By the 1770s, black New Englanders, thousands of whom were Revolutionary War veterans, had begun sending petitions to northern state legislatures demanding an end to slavery. These, essentially, worked. By the 1790s, ten states and territories, containing more than 50 percent of the free population of the new nation— Maine, New Hampshire, Vermont, Massachusetts, Rhode Island, Connecticut, New York, Pennsylvania, the Northwest Territory, and the Indiana Territory—were free land by law. And, the anti-slavery upswell continued apace.

In 1794, the U.S. Congress prohibited any participation by American ships in the Atlantic slave trade. In 1808, the Act Prohibiting Importation of Slaves took effect, making any shipment of enslaved persons from abroad into the U.S. a crime. Finally, in 1865, all slavery was declared to be illegal, at the constitutional level, in the United States. Since that latter milestone, the population of the country has grown 874 percent (38 million to 333 million) and our GDP has increased 11,796 percent ($15 billion to $18.638 trillion). Both increases were driven largely by modern-era foreign immigration.

Even within the South, even when it legally existed, there is little or no evidence that reliance on feudal serf labor made American slave states richer than their free counterparts. Rather, the opposite. Historian Marc Schulman has pointed out that, immediately before the Civil War, "the vast majority of industrial manufacturing" and other competitive industrial work was taking place in the North. In 1860, the South had about 25 percent of the United States' free white and black population, but "only 10 percent of the country's capital." The same was true for physical plants: the North had five times as many modern factories, and ten to twelve times as many trained factory workers. Overall, "at least 90 percent"[67] of the nation's skilled-trades workers were based in the North. In his book, *Black Rednecks and White Liberals,* economist Thomas Sowell goes a step beyond Schulman, arguing that the prevalence of slavery in the antebellum South resulted in a mocking and disparaging attitude toward hard work that continues to plague both "white trash" and inner-city black communities today.[68]

Of course, any cost-benefit analysis of the impact of slavery on the United States would be incomplete without including the costs of the war that freed the slaves. In dollar terms alone, the price tag for the Civil War was a high one. Between 1861 and 1865, the national debt of the United States surged from $65 million to $2.77 billion,[69] an increase of tens or hundreds of billions in today's dollars. However, even this pales in comparison to the great conflict's human toll. According to History.com's Jennie Cohen, the generally accepted figure for Union army battle deaths during the Civil War is 360,222. The equivalent figure for Confederate deaths, which many historians consider something of a lowball, is 258,000.[70]

All told, about one-tenth of the American men who were of military age in 1860 died as a direct result of the Civil War. Among specifically Southern white men in their early twenties, 22.6 percent—nearly one in four—died during the war. It seems no exaggeration to estimate that roughly one Union soldier died for every nine to ten slaves freed. If the U.S. owed a bill for slavery, we have, quite arguably, already paid it in blood.

A final point here is critical. To the activist political Left, troubles in the black community almost invariably are attributed to "the legacy of slavery," or to "racism" more broadly. However, the fatal flaw of this argument is that many such problems have worsened dramatically in recent years. Illegitimacy—out-of-wedlock child-bearing—is perhaps the most dramatic example of this. As the conservative black economist Walter Williams has pointed out, widespread illegitimacy within the black community is an almost entirely modern phenomenon. Back in 1925, in New York City and similar metropolitan areas, 85 percent[71] of black homes were headed up by stable two-parent families, a rate that persisted into the 1950s.

Even under slavery, Williams points out, "in up to three-quarters of the families, all children had the same mother and father." In contrast, the black illegitimacy rate today is 75 percent. It seems essentially impossible to attribute this to bigotry, given much less disturbing figures from past historical eras when racism was far worse. And illegitimacy does not stand alone as an outlier: African American rates of incarceration, drug use, STD infection, and unemployment all have been far worse[72] throughout most of the modern era than they were in 1950—or, one suspects, in 1925.

Empirically, contemporary factor variables such as pay-per-child welfare, no-fault divorce and the normalization of illegitimacy, under-policing of black neighborhoods, and the outsourcing of blue-collar jobs seem primarily responsible for contemporary problems in black communities—and poor white ones. Just maybe, we should focus on and discuss these factors as much as we do the ethnic conflicts of two hundred years ago.

In sum, the 1619 Project is correct that slavery is an existential horror. However, this practice was not some unique moral failure on the part of the United States. Slavery was the norm everywhere in the world until Western societies began to fight to end it, and the large majority of America's slaves were purchased from powerful West African and Arab slave traders "of color." Further, historical slavery did not shape most of the modern institutions of American society. The American region reliant on slave labor was by far the poorest in the country, and almost seven hundred thousand lives were lost when we conquered it and freed the slaves.

Finally, today's problems in American minority communities—most of which, by the way, are doing rather well—often have nothing whatsoever to do with the atrocities of 154 years ago. Ironically, more than a few of them seem to be the result of "compassionate" liberal social welfare policies implemented during just the past few decades. As in virtually every other context, it is not hard to take an ethical position on slavery that is to the right of the *New York Times*.

"BLACK IS THE NEW IDOL"
BY YAYA J. FANUSIE

Black is an idol now. It is worshipped. The black race is the "Black" race now, according to the *New York Times*,[73] the Associated Press,[74] and other media outlets. And "black is king," according to the title of Beyoncé's new musical film that streamed on Disney Plus. Beyoncé is an artistic genius, and I will not judge a film I've yet to see, but the title is peculiarly provocative for Disney. It seems rather tone-deaf in a pluralistic society.

My main concern, however, is not with what non-African Americans think about how we express our identity, but about how our self-identity impacts our growth as a people. "Black is king" seems to be a nod to African and African American greatness, or as Beyoncé describes it, "the beauty of tradition and Black excellence." But appeals to "black greatness"[75] without acknowledging the importance of morality can lead us away from the human freedom and advancement our ancestors struggled for if we're not careful. It may be unpopular today to question these assertive expressions for self-esteem, but my own personal journey urges me to do so.

As a teenager in the late 1980s and early '90s, I was hyper-focused on race and blackness. In high school, to demonstrate my militant love of black identity, I regularly wore a black jacket and a black leather baseball cap with a red, black, and green Africa pin on the side. It was the golden age of hip hop, and I loved writing rap lyrics. My signature rhyme back then was called "Raise your mind to Blackness." Looking back, I see that time as an important period of awakening for me, when I gained an appreciation of my heritage and developed greater awareness of the historical and contemporary struggles of the African American situation.

This emphasis on black pride was my counterweight to address the remnants of racism I saw in 1980s and '90s America. Some of those remnants manifested as incidents close to home, such as the Rodney King beating, which occurred a few blocks from my house at the time. Much of it was from what I viewed on television, such as the famous *Oprah Winfrey Show* episode[76] in 1987, when Oprah visited a Georgia county that had banned African American residents since 1912.

In reaction to such realities, I embraced a "too black, too strong" identity. Like many teenage awakenings, the orientation I took on was a bit imbalanced. I'm thankful for the growth of that period, but it came with a cost. Blackness became my barometer for what was correct, what was worthwhile, and what was good. I would never have used these words at the time, but what I embraced was essentially a morality for ethnicity. There is a fine line between appreciating your culture and being obsessed with it.

Something changed by the late 1990s to help me evolve. After years steeped in what was essentially a worship of my race and culture, I went through a new awakening, a spiritual one. I had been reading an English translation of the Qur'an daily, contemplating converting to Islam. At one point in my reading, I reached a verse that said: "O mankind! We created you from a single (pair) of a male and a female, and made you into nations and tribes, that ye may know each other (not that ye may despise (each other) [sic]. Verily the most honoured of you in the sight of Allah is (he who is) the most righteous of you."[77]

It was a seminal moment. Instantly, and for the first time, I began to question a longstanding assumption I held—that, because of the existence of anti-black racism in the world, black racial pride was a sufficient and noble goal by itself. Those Quranic words challenged that notion. They conveyed quite elegantly that race, culture, and heritage had little value when detached from morality. Culture could be beautiful, but it was utilitarian and meant to help us orient ourselves evenly with other cultures and peoples, all under God. I was humbled.

Making black our "king" reminds me of when I urged my high school friends to "raise their minds to blackness." It was a push to pride without any prescription of conduct. But this is more problematic today than in my youth. In the '80s and '90s our pro-black assertions and callouts of racism were not mutually exclusive to reminders of personal conduct. Consider two popular hip-hop songs of that era, "We're All in the Same Gang"[78] and "Self-Destruction."[79] The biggest rappers of the day came together on those records to discourage black-on-black crime. Also think about Boogie Down Productions' "Love's Gonna Get'cha,"[80] which narrates the story of a young African American whose love of material wealth leads to his rise as a drug dealer, violence against his family, and his eventual death or arrest.

Today's popular African American thought leaders would frame such messages as nothing more than blaming the victim and pandering to so-called white supremacy. Yet, back then, we could criticize "the system" and our own community members' actions without being denigrated. Now, most of our cultural expressions of social consciousness emphasize only the outer circumstances and stay mute on our inner conduct. Both conservatives and liberals are vulnerable to backlash. As far back as 2013, President Obama drew heat from voices in the African American community for telling recent Morehouse College graduates to make no excuses for themselves and embrace personal responsibility[81] as they went out into the world.

It is a shame that our African American intelligentsia reflexively eschew any appeal to morality as misguided "respectability politics"[82] and frame it as an attempt for elusive white acceptance. However, self-respect, if it means anything, has little to do with how others see you. And it is odd since it is undeniable that religion with strong moral codes was central to African American progress throughout our centuries-long struggle for freedom. Our ancestors who were the most successful in building African American justice, education, and empowerment were believers in religious scripture, and thus valued a self-identity beyond their skin color, even when their color was central to their struggle.

Frederick Douglass was not struggling for blackness. He was struggling for blacks, influenced by what he called "the Christianity of Christ"[83] that he read in the Bible, rather than the warped version he experienced in slave-holding America. Harriet Tubman was not emboldened to free people by her blackness. She was emboldened by her deep belief in God[84] to take the risks she took. Marcus Garvey, well known for spurring thousands of followers toward racial unity, pride, and self-determination, was what might today be called "unapologetically Christian." His "Back to Africa" movement had a strong missionary component[85] that later Pan-African admirers dismissed.

As a Muslim, I see a parallel in the role of my faith in our history. Many do not get how our Muslim African American leaders of the past were pushing for a universal, moral identity. Malcolm X is characterized one-dimensionally for black nationalism, but he despised the term "Black Muslim," even when he was building the Nation of Islam. He stressed this in his autobiography, commenting on how the news media wrongly latched onto the term "Black Muslims": "The public mind fixed on 'Black Muslims.' From Mr. [Elijah] Muhammad on down, the name 'Black Muslims' distressed everyone in the Nation of Islam. I tried for at least two years to kill off that 'Black Muslims.' Every newspaper and magazine writer and microphone I got close to [I told]: 'No! We are black people here in America. Our religion is Islam. We are properly called 'Muslims'!" But that 'Black Muslim' name never got dislodged."

Malcolm in both his Nation of Islam and post-NOI days tried to help African Americans tap an identity of an inner nature, which is difficult to do when using terminology that emphasizes something solely external, such as skin color. Though the Nation of Islam pushed an idea of black supremacy, its catechisms taught that black people's true nature that they must rediscover was that of a "righteous Muslim." Nobility was not in color by itself. It is noteworthy that after his pilgrimage to Makkah, El-Hajj Malik El-Shabazz started a group which he named the Organization of Afro-American Unity,[86] not the Organization of Black Unity.

And after NOI leader Elijah Muhammad died in 1975, his son Imam W. D. Mohammed was selected to lead the movement. He then directed his following to embrace universal Islam and steer away from color language. For a brief time, the former NOI community called itself "Bilalian,"[87] in honor of Bilal ibn Rabah, the brown-skinned Abyssinian who embraced Islam as a slave, became free, and was a beloved companion of Muhammad the Prophet. Imam W. D. Mohammed's association emphasized that they saw themselves simply as Muslim Americans and would specify "African American Muslims" only to be precise when necessary. Color-focused nomenclature was rejected, as was a race-based worldview.[88]

How times have changed in a short period! It is not insignificant that "black" has overtaken "African American" as the media's preferred descriptor of Americans with recent African ancestry. "Black" conveys a subtly different spirit, rooted in the topical aesthetic and serving as a binary opponent to "whiteness." Still, the phrase "black is beautiful" is passé now. That self-esteem-invoking mantra seemed necessary in an era when Beyoncé's or Lupita Nyong'o's beauty would be uncelebrated by America's mainstream media. But today's mantras are provocative hashtags and memes. Our new generation asserts that they are unapologetically #BlackAF, because they don't give two Fs what you think about their blackness.

I am sure "black is king" will be a stunningly beautiful exposition of African and African American culture. But I wonder what it will point us toward. My worry is that it will call us to find nobility attached so much to our color, when that is the most superficial aspect of ourselves. I am concerned it will urge us to think of our culture as honorable, but with no standard beyond aesthetics. Black pride is certainly an important part of our growth. But if it is all that guides us, we certainly will be stunted.

"THE HISTORY OF 1776 OFFERS HOPE FOR ALL AMERICANS"
BY REV. COREY BROOKS

The beautiful story of America's Founding, the most radical experiment in self-government and individual liberty, is becoming lost in an agenda-driven narrative.

By now, most Americans are aware of the 1619 Project, a political project of the *New York Times* aimed at rewriting America's Founding. The project weaves together a divisive narrative not only about the foundation of our nation, but also our country's core principles.

An unfortunate consequence of this rewrite of our nation's history is that this project excludes the possibility of redemption—at both the national level and the individual level. The primary problem with the 1619 Project is a pervasive one that runs throughout the entire presentation—namely, the over-emphasis on slavery as the defining institution before and during our nation's founding. The writers who participated in the project jettisoned facts in favor of a fictitious recounting of why our Founders formed a new nation. From the 1619 Project's perspective, the overarching motivation behind the founding of the United States of America was the desire to expand slavery.

Criticizing the 1619 Project's flawed methodology and conclusions is not to excuse slavery. Slavery is, without a doubt, one of the most complicated and tragic aspects of American history. That our Founders, who strived so diligently to break free from the bonds of the British crown, could allow—and, in many cases, participate in—the evil institution of slavery is a blight on our history and a deep moral failing on their part. The Founders' letters[89] to one another offer glimpses for us so we see how much they struggled with the inconsistencies of slavery and this new political experiment.

But one need not be an apologist for slavery to find fault with the 1619 Project's myopic view of the founding. "Our democracy's founding ideals were false when they were written," reads the headline of the 1619 Project essay.[90] This statement merely reflects the authors' misguided understanding of the power of our founding ideals.

The Declaration of Independence, one of the most important political documents ever produced, contains this key passage: "We hold these truths to be self-evident, that all men are created equal, that they are endowed by their Creator with certain unalienable rights, that among these are life, liberty and the pursuit of happiness. That to secure these rights, governments are instituted among men, deriving their just powers from the consent of the governed."[91]

Is slavery compatible with the ideal that all men are created equal? Of course not.

Is slavery compatible with the recognition that we have God-given rights, chief among them life, liberty, and the pursuit of happiness? Definitely not.

Slavery is the most egregious example where we, as a nation, failed to implement and execute the vision for a government of free individuals. Many of our Founders understood this inconsistency and fought to abolish slavery from the start. Slavery's existence at our founding is commentary on the frailty of those individuals who participated in slave ownership, not on the hollowness of our founding documents.

The overarching theme of our founding documents is the possibility of what the individual can achieve, thanks to his or her freedom. We often call it the American Dream. It is the heart and soul of our nation's mission statement.

As a pastor on the South Side of Chicago, I see the effects of racism, but I also see the effects of missing out on the American Dream. That missed opportunity comes in many forms—as a result of rampant black-on-black violence, the self-defeating bonds of thinking of ourselves as victims, and avoiding rewarding hard work.

Project H.O.O.D.,[92] a program I founded on the South Side of Chicago as a ministry of our church, offers a path forward out of poverty that is rooted in the American Dream. Part of our goal through our ministry programs, of course, is to help people find freedom in Jesus Christ. At the same time, we also show them the freedom that comes from participating in the American Dream, the most empowering economic opportunity there is. Through our programs, I have seen many lives changed. And they were changed because the individuals saw themselves as part of—not excluded from—the American Dream.

Working directly with former gang members, we provide a course correction in their lives. If they want something better for themselves and their families, we offer valuable jobs training in the areas of construction, lawn care, and trucking. We have seen young men go from being part of some of the nation's most violent gangs to bringing home steady paychecks in their new careers—and loving the freedom that comes with their independent life.

The story of Jonathan Watkins is a powerful reminder of how a life can be turned around. In all of my years of ministry, Jonathan's story is the most horrifying one I have ever witnessed, but, because of the extreme sadness, the redemption of his life is all the more joyful.

Jonathan was twenty-nine years old and had a six-month-old baby girl in 2013. He stole a video game system, and once the owner of the system found out, he came to Jonathan's house with a gun. Seeing Jonathan in a car, he began shooting at the car. Tragically, one of the bullets struck Jonathan's little daughter, Jonylah, and she died the following day in the hospital.

Over the past seven years, Jonathan has had to make a concrete decision: Would he continue down his path, with all of the destructive violence, or would he do the hard work of pursuing a new plan? I am pleased to say Jonathan made the better choice and is an inspiration to others. I have had the privilege of mentoring Jonathan, and he is now pursuing his GED. He works with Project H.O.O.D. to do violence intervention and training.

Another uplifting story about an individual who embraced the empowering opportunities associated with the American Dream is Billy Kelly. Billy served time in prison but now owns Panda Construction, a multimillion-dollar Chicago-based business, and he has helped give others in the community the opportunity to gain skills and jobs in the construction industry. Billy's personal success story has multiplied to become hundreds of other black individuals' own success stories, as they work through his training programs and gain steady employment.

Varney Voker, once of the notorious Black Disciples gang, over-saw a highly sophisticated drug-dealing operation on Chicago's South Side for many years until he was convicted. Upon his exit from prison, he returned to Woodlawn, where I had since set up shop. I challenged Varney to use his experience to help other youth in Woodlawn avoid his path. He is now one of our best mentors and runs a successful logistics company.

That's why Project H.O.O.D. exists. We want to magnify these individual success stories. Our vision is to end violence and build communities, one neighborhood at a time. We equip youths, adults, and families with the resources, skills, and tools they need to harness their own American Dream success story. We often say, "We seek to empower, not enable. We seek to equip, not excuse. We seek to inform, not ignore."

Political projects such as the 1619 Project do nothing to help black Americans escape the noxious "us-versus-them" mentality, and they rob generations of Americans of the power of the American Dream.

I have discovered on the South Side of Chicago that the absolute best way to overcome racial disparities in economic and academic outcomes is to teach individuals about the incredible opportunities of being in America—not to fixate on the mistakes of the past. Personal responsibility, an American concept closely linked to individual freedom, is the ticket to a turned-around life.

"RESPONSES TO ADVERSITY"
BY ROBERT CHERRY

The *New York Times'* 1619 Project has focused on linking the extreme harshness of slavery to the black experience of today. But overstating this link is misleading. It promotes inaccurate representations of the behaviors of the enslaved and reinforces contemporary negative stereotypes that are simply inaccurate if one examines various aspects of the black family, marriage rates, and other data that reflect strong ethics of black slaves in both moral and economic terms during the most sinful chapter in American history.

The 1619 Project's Matthew Desmond's essay[93] suggests—accurately—that slavery was a vicious system of exploitation, a perception found in influential early post-World War II writings. In *Slavery: A Problem in American Institutional and Intellectual Life*,[94] Stanley Elkins claims that the long series of shocks from their African capture, Middle Passage transport to the West Indies, and sale to American plantations created a black psyche similar to what Bruno Bettelheim observed[95] in Nazi concentration camps. Elkins believed that typical enslaved blacks would adopt a childlike quality of complete submission, identifying their masters as father figures since "their real fathers had virtually no authority over their children." This thesis was Elkins's explanation for the "Little Black Sambo" image that once was widely accepted among researchers and observers of the slave experience.

In *The Peculiar Institution*,[96] Kenneth Stampp believed that terror and brutalization were at the core of the slave experience. As a result, an enslaved black understood that to be the recipient of his master's paternalism, he had to adopt the pose of "a fawning dependent," producing a "process of infantilization."[97] Furthermore, Stampp claimed that family values were so destroyed that most fathers and even some mothers regarded their children with indifference.

Although Elkins and Stampp saw themselves as exposing the inhumanities of slavery, they, unfortunately, reinforced negative images of enslaved men and women—that enslaved blacks lacked a strong work ethic, lacked a strong commitment to the nuclear family, and lacked sexual discipline. For W. E. B. Dubois, later E. Franklin Frazier, and ultimately, Daniel Patrick Moynihan, their work explained the high rate of black births out of wedlock.

This led many whites to consider black laborers as inherently lazy and requiring stern discipline to harness their work effort. The leading early twentieth-century labor economist John R. Commons believed that "the backward nonwhite races were lazy, could not compete, and therefore did not need unions."[98] There continues to be a widespread belief that too many black men lack a strong work ethic.[99]

In the 1970s, Herbert Gutman, Robert Fogel, and Eugene Genovese undermined the Stampp-Elkins thesis. Using Freedmen's Bureau data and records from six large plantations, Gutman found that more than three-quarters of all children were raised in stable, two-parent families. This outcome reflected the fact that fewer than one in five marriages was ended as a result of the slave trade. Family stability was lower on plantations with fewer than fifteen slaves. Still, in these smaller plantations, half of the enslaved children grew up in two-parent families.

Slave women still fell victim to white men's lust. However, according to Genovese, "many escaped because the whites knew they had black men who would rather die than stand idly by." So strong was the resistance that it curbed "white sexual aggression" against married women.

For these researchers, the plantation owner's absolute control was tempered by a primary focus on profitability. Since prime-age enslaved males were costly to purchase, planters took care to not risk their safety. Slaves were whipped and sexually abused, but not employed on high-risk activities when possible. Instead, the plantation owners hired Irish immigrants, who were considered "disposable," to do these dangerous jobs.

For slavers, the hiring of white overseers was expensive. Fogel found that they were employed on only one-sixth of moderate-size plantations (sixteen to fifty slaves) and 25 to 30 percent on larger ones. On three-quarters of plantations with no white overseers, there was only one adult male of working age. This required extensive employment of enslaved blacks in supervisory positions, as well as in many craft positions.

Since white supervision was expensive, and it was expensive to purchase slaves, planters found it profitable to provide positive inducements to instill loyalty and improve work efforts. Genovese found that masters who practiced paternalism were more successful than those who used their powers ruthlessly. Ex-slave narratives indicated that stealing was much higher on the plantations that provided meager rations.

Positive incentives took many forms. On many plantations, enslaved workers who performed well were awarded private plots of land on which they could farm and sell their surplus. Fogel estimated that "income of top field hands was 2.5 times basic income; of top craftsmen, probably four or five, and in some exceptional cases, as much as 10 times basic income."

Not only was the Stampp-Elkins view wrong about the place of the nuclear family in slave lives, it was wrong about the black work ethic. As mentioned, enslaved blacks were employed in many skilled and semi-skilled positions. In the agricultural sector, Fogel estimated 20 percent of enslaved blacks were employed in management, skilled artisan, and semi-skilled positions. As a result, the early twentieth-century researcher Charles Wesley claimed that at emancipation, black workers made up over 80 percent of the artisan class in the South.[100] Indeed, in *The Negro Artisan*,[101] DuBois commented on the potpourri of occupations available to black workers in the South, compared to the North, where craft unions almost universally embraced racial exclusionary practices.

Fogel lamented the mistaken view of black labor by slavery critics: "That the quality of slaves…could have been so completely misrepresented…is testimony to the extent of their racist myopia. What bitter irony it is that the false stereotype of black labor, a stereotype which still plagues blacks today, was fashioned not primarily by the oppressors…but by the most ardent opponents of slavery, by those who worked most diligently to destroy the chains of bondage."

Similar to the Stampp-Elkins narrative, some observers today stress the impact of deeply rooted oppressive circumstances. Besides ongoing violence perpetuated by racist policing, they emphasize deep intergenerational poverty. They point to Patrick Sharkey's estimates that 67 percent of black American families hailing from the poorest quarter of neighborhoods a generation ago continue to live in such neighborhoods today.[102] Among all black families, 48 percent have lived in poor neighborhoods for at least two generations, compared to only 7 percent of white families.

These deplorable conditions, we are told, create pervasive hopelessness. According to researchers Melissa Kearney and Kathryn Edin, the high levels of teen pregnancies that have afflicted the black community are the result of a "culture of despair." Hopelessness presumably explained the causal sexuality that Ta-Nehisi Coates witnessed growing up in Baltimore in the 1980s. "Lexington Terrace was hot with gonorrhea. Teen pregnancy was the fashion," he wrote in *The Beautiful Struggle*. "Husbands were outies. Fathers were ghosts."[103]

Unfortunately, the liberal position is based on a misreading of contemporary behaviors, just as the severest critics of U.S. slavery misread the behavior of enslaved blacks. The "culture of despair" explanation for high teen birth rates ignores the role of predatory male behavior. Typical of the decade, in 1993, 20.9 percent of black teen girls became pregnant, 7.8 percent had abortions, and 10.7 percent gave birth. At that time, many poor black girls who lacked employment sought money by hooking up with problematic men. Patricia Collins documented how "young women engage in casual sex with men" with the "unstated assumptions that they will be rewarded with a little financial help."[104] Some scholars have suggested[105] that unwanted black pregnancies were strongly associated with younger teens entering coercive sexual relationships with older men. My own study[106] with Chun Wang found that states with high employment rates of twenty to twenty-four-year-olds also had higher rates of birth among fifteen to nineteen-year-olds.

You, however, would be unaware that teen pregnancy reflected these abusive and coercive relationships if you had read only Kathryn Edin's books. None of the teen mothers who dominated her two books—*Making Ends Meet* and *Promises I Can Keep*—were victims of coercive or predatory males. Neither did the intimate violence so prevalent in poor black neighborhoods appear in her work. Not surprisingly, she was quite willing to "highlight how growing up in an environment where there is little chance of social and economic advancement can lead young women to have babies outside of marriage."[107]

In support of the "culture of despair" thesis, Phillip Levine and Melissa Kearney found that, on average, states with higher levels of income inequality had high rates of teen births.[108] As employment plummeted during the Great Recession, the "despair thesis" would have predicted teen birth rates to rise. Instead, they decreased by 44 percent between 2006 and 2014.[109]

One of the important reasons for this decline was the growing educational attainment of black women. Rather than being trapped in despair, increasingly they sought to better their lives through education that freed them from problematic black men. Between 2006 and 2015, the share of black women ages twenty-five to twenty-nine with at least an associate's degree rose by 28.1 percent.[110] As a result, black adolescent women had reason to believe they could attain educational credentials to better their lives, so they rejected teen motherhood.

We should not trivialize the deprivation and discrimination black Americans have faced. Nor should we ignore the debilitating effects of some of their experiences. However, we should limit the victim narrative and, instead, focus on the broader evidence that many have triumphed over these roadblocks.

"THE CULT OF VICTIMHOOD"
BY HAROLD A. BLACK

Those who insist that slavery is the root of all evil in America and that, as a result, blacks are victims denigrate the strength of black Americans. I long have argued that, contrary to the designation of those who grew up during the Great Depression and fought in World War II as the "Greatest Generation," in reality the greatest generation was that of the freed slaves. These were people who had been demeaned as chattel and had no possessions; many had no marketable skills, were mostly illiterate, and lacked a last name. They were suddenly liberated from southern plantations and thrust into the world of freedom.

Certainly, many were transformed from slaves into tenant farmers, but at least they were free. Many were exploited, but many also received an education provided by whites who founded a number of our black colleges. Indeed, Howard University is named for Union Gen. Oliver O. Howard, who commanded a wing of Sherman's army and who my great-grandmother told me "came up Bonner's Hill" in Clinton, Georgia, while she was picking cotton. I find it hard to believe that Howard, Spelman, and Morehouse colleges were founded by whites to victimize blacks.

Those who insist on according blacks victim status are guilty of perpetuating the caricatures of black people made famous by Stepin Fetchit,[111] *Little Black Sambo, Uncle Tom's Cabin,* and *Mandingo.* Given that caricatures are parodies, victimhood is little more than an excuse.

Convincing some that they cannot achieve because they are black flies in the face of this paradox: How can a high-achieving black person truthfully tell another black person that their lack of achievement is because of their race?

I grew up with parents who, because of their upbringing, neither tolerated excuses nor believed in victimhood. We lived in southwest Atlanta's all-black enclave. As a result, I never had a conversation with a white person until I became the first black male freshman at the University of Georgia in 1966. For us, whites were a caricature. We saw them through the lens of the television. Shows such as *The Adventures of Ozzie and Harriet* showed us a household to which we could not relate because the wife did not work outside the home. Through the news, we saw images of white women cursing and spitting on black children trying to go to school in Clinton, Tennessee, and Little Rock, Arkansas, and the horrifying images of Emmett Till's beaten body and, later, those of James Chaney, Andrew Goodman, and Michael Schwerner. These events and others reinforced the feeling among my peers that most whites were violent, uneducated, and best avoided.

My first day on campus, these feelings quickly dissipated when I met white students, who became my friends despite some name-calling and ostracizing from their peers.

Across the changes in economic status from my former-slave great-grandparents to my grandparents to my parents and to me, a retired finance professor with a PhD, and my late brother, a former airline pilot with a PhD, I cannot find one victim. Nor can I find a victim among any of my other relatives.

My father was from a small town in south Georgia. His parents did not finish high school. His mother was a "domestic" and would not let her four girls do household chores; the three boys did them instead. She said she did not want her girls to have to work in white people's houses and insisted that all her children go to college. They did. Six of them graduated, and the seventh became a businessman.

My maternal grandfather was a farmer, working land that had been in the family since 1868. My grandmother had a high school education and served as the one-room schoolmarm for black children in their rural Georgia county.

No one among my relatives on either side considered himself or herself a victim.

As a result, I never dreamed of telling my parents about any of the incidents that occurred during my freshman year as the first—and only—black male living in a dorm. I knew that I could not come into the house with "C" marks saying the average grades were because someone would break my windows most nights and I could not study. My father would have said, "Then find a place to study." So I did. No excuses. No whining. No victims.

Nevertheless, growing up in the segregated South prompted me to ask my parents why they didn't leave. Until my college years, though largely left alone if they "knew their place," blacks in the South endured a reign of terror. A black person could be killed by a white who was not likely to be prosecuted. Indeed, two of my mother's cousins were lynched in 1913, and their killers were never arrested. Yet my parents and others like them did not leave because of a strong sense of home—and a stronger sense that they would not be better off living in the North.

Some did leave. Nicholas Lemann's wonderful *The Promised Land: The Great Black Migration and How It Changed America* could have been the story of those in my family who left Jones County, Georgia, for Detroit to work in the factories during World War II. My maternal grandfather also left but returned shortly after because he could not find any rabbits to hunt. The Yankee cousins would visit in their big cars and fur coats, mocking their country cousins who tilled the soil on hardscrabble farms. They pitied us because their children matriculated at the University of Michigan and Michigan State while we were relegated to meagerly supported, segregated state colleges. My father went to Savannah State, and my mother was the first four-year graduate of Fort Valley State University.

Much like my grandfather, my parents also preferred living in the segregated South. My father's own work conditions were more or less integrated. His full-time night job was as a clerk at the main post office. But this was the only place where his colleagues could be white and the bathrooms and lunchroom were not segregated. He always resented that only his black coworkers had college degrees and none of the whites did except for the supervisors. In those days, in the Deep South, blacks with college degrees could only work for themselves or for the government. However, my parents simply could not envision the circumstances under which blacks would want to live with whites, and especially worship with them.

This was a time in the South when, as an educated person, you could have a good life and live comfortably if you "kept to your place." We lived among blacks in a middle-class neighborhood. We were mostly two-adult households and college-educated. The yards were well kept. There was no litter; if a piece of trash somehow found its way into our neighborhood, we would stop the car and pick it up.

All of us kids went to college. Most went to black colleges, but some, like my brother, who wanted to be an engineer, went away. He went to Purdue instead of Georgia Tech because, when he graduated from Booker T. Washington High School in 1960, no black state school offered degrees in engineering and the state of Georgia gave him a tuition stipend to leave the state. My parents fully expected us to return home after acquiring our education. When my brother became a pilot, it was no surprise that he diligently worked to make Atlanta his home base. It took him several years, but when it happened, he moved into an all-black neighborhood close to the airport.

Throughout my family's history we have been guided by choice and responsibility, not by victimhood. Therefore, the notion of reparations for slavery puzzles me. The answer, of course, lies in the cult of victimhood that seeks to trivialize the stunning accomplishments of our people from the day they set foot in America to their proud descendants.

The issue of reparations is not new. In 1999, several African nations demanded that the West pay $777 trillion in reparations.[112] This argument was curious, in that many if not most Africans were sold into slavery by other Africans. In 2004, the British government was sued for reparations for its role in the slave trade. Nothing was paid, but the British prime minister apologized[113] for Britain's participation in the slave trade. In the Caribbean, many nations also demanded reparations to no avail.

The problem of payment is an issue unto itself. If individual blacks were to be compensated, there would be a problem of equity. Surely individuals such as Tiger Woods and LeBron James would not receive payments that were the same as those paid to the indigent. Questions would arise as to who was black and whose ancestors were slaves. There would be a rush on DNA studies as whites would seek to be classified as black.

As a case in point, a dear friend of mine while conducting an ancestor search discovered to her surprise that her great-grandmother was classified as mulatto in an early census. Should she receive compensation?

In my case, my mother's DNA revealed that she was 32 percent British and less than 50 percent African. In my case, I am over 50 percent African with the rest being British, Scots-Irish, Western European, and Scandinavian. Thus, instead of being African American, I guess I should be reclassified as mongrel American. Suggestions that reparations go to institutions or certain charities also are rife with flaws. It truly is difficult to envision compensating some for the sins of others' ancestors. Still, if there is really such a thing as white guilt, then I would be happy to receive any money they might want to send me, though as a matter of law, I consider it ridiculous.

There actually have been reparations aplenty. The War on Poverty has spent over \$23 trillion in reparations since 1965.[114] Although some on the Right point out that poverty rates are unchanged, and those on the Left say that this means trillions more must be spent, both are wrong. Grants and subsidies are not counted as income. If they were, poverty rates would fall to less than 5 percent, indicating a lessening of poverty. Moreover, when I look at the household income of blacks, I also see that reparations have been paid. Yes, the mean black household income of \$59,000 is significantly less than that of whites (\$89,000), but compare that to the per capita income of the three African countries in my DNA: Cameroon, \$1,451; Mali, \$827; and Togo, \$610.

So even though slavery was evil, cruel, and harsh, we are a proud people who have prospered despite the odds. We are only hampered when we listen to people who demean us by insisting that racism prevents us from being full participants in society, despite all the evidence to the contrary. Read *John Sibley Butler's Entrepreneurship and Self-Help among Black Americans: A Reconsideration of Race and Economics*, and then consider that it was the War on Poverty's resultant destruction of the black family that derailed our progress. Although some may think that the War on Poverty was intended to make blacks wards of the state, and that this is the real victimization, many blacks have not succumbed to it and have continued to send their children to schools, to take their families to church, and to teach self-responsibility.

We all know that poverty rates are dramatically higher among single-mother households. More than 77 percent of black children are born out of wedlock. Marriage drops the probability of child poverty by 82 percent.[115] Moreover, there is a significant gap in the incomes of college-educated households and other households regardless of race.

Blacks have a proud history of strength and self-reliance. That continues today, despite the caricatures painted by those demanding reparations. I am reminded of a student of mine who was wearing a T-shirt depicting a black person in chains with the words "I was not asked to be brought here." I asked her, "Aren't you glad you were?" Her answer was, "Oh, my goodness, yes!" So I repeat: reparations aplenty.

"LIVING BY THE GRACE OF GOD AND THE POWER OF APPLYING ONESELF"
BY DEAN NELSON

When I was in third grade, my parents, who both worked in Washington, DC, were finally able to build a house in their rural hometown of Marshall, Virginia. We had been living inside the Beltway in an apartment, but they were willing to brave the commute from Marshall so that my sisters and I could be cared for after school by my grandmother, who lived down the hill. My one sister insists they made this move because someone tried to kidnap her, but I've never been entirely clear about that story.

As the house neared completion, someone needed to prepare the acre of surrounding land for grass seed, and that someone was me. Eight years young, I was handed a large contraption made up of eight two-by-fours nailed together in a square, with scores of long nails driven through them. This homemade plow attached to a long strap that went across my chest. For hours upon hours, I walked the length of what would become our lawn, dragging the two-by-fours behind me, the long nails breaking up the ground. In the years that followed, I would mow the grass that grew there for hours every week, along with doing landscaping and other chores for elderly neighbors for a few bucks.

Today, my son is responsible for mowing the postage stamp-sized patch in front of our home, for which I occasionally give him money. It takes him about fifteen minutes if he does a really good job. This disparity between our childhood experiences might help explain why so many people my children's age seem to measure racial progress by how offended they feel on any given day. It's much easier to ponder your offenses when you are lying on the couch in the air conditioning.

If light manual labor played an irreplaceable role in forming my character, I understood it simply as part of growing up. Grown-ups worked, and if I wanted to be one, I had better start learning how. (Despite the relative lack of manual labor in the suburbs, my own kids have worked steadily from the time they were legally allowed to.) My grandparents did not have air conditioning or indoor plumbing until I was ten, but I never thought of them as poor. I loved playing at their house, although I was relieved to learn that the house my parents built did indeed have flushing toilets.

My idyllic childhood, surrounded by a large and loving extended family, did not mean that I didn't see or experience racism. I heard the "N-word" as a matter of course. There was a restaurant in our town that refused service to blacks well into the 1980s. As children, my cousin and I were chased into the woods by a white man with a shotgun. (We had been throwing snowballs at cars, which was wrong. But even by the standards of the day, this was an overreaction.) My school guidance counselor told me not to take Latin (she said I would fail) and suggested that I enlist in the military instead of applying to college. At no time during my childhood did my parents, who attended segregated schools, or my grandparents, who did not even attend high school, say anything negative to me about whites.

Only later in life did I interpret my guidance counselor's advice as a possible example of subconscious racial bias. At the time, when I brought the idea of joining the military to my mother, she informed me that I would not be enlisting and that I would, in fact, be going to college. Neither she nor my father had four-year degrees, but this was what they expected of me. I don't remember it feeling like a burden, but I do remember that I trusted my mother's opinion of my capabilities more than that of my guidance counselor.

When I was younger, my mother had bought me a series of children's biographies of black historical figures that included all the familiar faces: Martin Luther King Jr., Harriet Tubman, George Washington Carver, and so on. But the one that caught my attention the most was Frederick Douglass, because two of the thin volumes were devoted to him. He must have been particularly important, I thought, to merit two books instead of one. And anyone who has read much about Mr. Douglass would agree that he packed at least two lifetimes of accomplishments into his seventy-seven years.

What a man! Even as an elementary schooler, I could discern that he must have been a formidable figure. Every portrait of him—even the pencil sketches on the front of my books—exuded dignity and demanded respect. Here was someone who taught himself to read, escaped slavery, and went on to advise one of the most important presidents! If he began in slavery and accomplished all that, surely the possibilities for me were endless.

What I was learning from my parents, grandparents, Mr. Douglass, and all the other subjects of those biographies—without realizing it at the time—was how to deal with racism without losing my sense of who I was or absorbing racial insults into my soul. This is not to say that those who feel wounded by racism are to blame for their wounds. My experiences, including the ones I have had in adulthood, have been extremely mild compared to those of many of my friends. But I have also met many people who have experienced less overt racism than I have, who nonetheless feel haunted by the opinions of whites and hopeless about the prospects for black people in our country. Each new incident captured on video or splashed across the headlines causes them further despair. Why is this?

I was first introduced to something like the thinking behind the 1619 Project narrative when I was a freshman at Howard University in the mid-1980s. Never before had it occurred to me to process the racial slights I experienced as personal affronts. I knew they were wrong, of course, but I had never thought of "people being ignorant" as a serious injustice in need of correction. But I was a country boy, easily impressed by my more sophisticated urban peers. They seemed to know all this information about racism that I had never heard before. Their explanations of how difficult it was for black people to get ahead stirred feelings of outrage in me that I previously had not experienced. It was intoxicating.

When I went back home for the holidays that winter, I started viewing little slights in an entirely new way. The ignorant white people I encountered were no longer just harmless buffoons. They were now "powerful oppressors" holding me back and keeping me down. And somehow this new set of beliefs was supposed to combat the notion of white supremacy.

After getting better grades at Howard than I had gotten throughout high school, I transferred to the University of Virginia for my sophomore year. If I had been prone to develop an inferiority complex, the grades I earned that first year at UVA surely would have pushed me over the edge. The easiest response in the world would have been to conclude that my plummeting grade point average was just another link in the chain of white oppression that had kept my ancestors enslaved and my parents in segregated schools.

Instead—by the grace of God—I was able to dig into that same force that enabled me to break up that acre of fallow Virginia clay at eight years old. I dragged my behind to the library for more hours each day than I previously had thought humanly possible. My aptitude for learning, thinking, and writing rose, as did my GPA, and I graduated on time. In that process, I also decided that ignorant whites were no longer going to command my attention. I decided instead that I would do all I could to improve the situation of blacks in our country. I wanted as many black Americans as possible to enjoy the incredible advantages I had so far in life: faith in God, a loving, stable family, a good education, and seemingly limitless opportunities to put it to use.

I am a grassroots guy, not a scholar, so I will not try to engage the 1619 Project from an academic point of view. What I can tell you is that I—and the thousands of African American pastors and leaders I am privileged to serve—learned in our schools the very "white history" that the 1619 Project seeks to remedy. Like me, most of the ministers I know had their public school education supplemented by additional black achievement-oriented reading material and black history-focused church events.[116] Like the books given to me by my mother, that material and those events depicted black Americans as leaders who triumphed over adversity and made the country a better place, not as victims who led lives of tragic desperation.

Learning "white history" in school did not cause any of us to believe we were inferior to anyone, nor did we somehow naively conclude that the world was free of racism. The racism we did experience did not make us think that America and its ideals didn't belong to us, nor did it deprive us of the ability to love our country and work to make it better. And thankfully, we did not enter adulthood looking for pity or thinking of ourselves as helpless pawns in a white man's world.

My organization, Douglass Leadership Institute, named for Frederick Douglass, works on issues of importance to black churchgoers, which include strengthening the black family, supporting criminal justice reform, and securing economic and educational opportunities for all. In our work on the black family, we have found that there are two opposite dangers that black parents must avoid when teaching their children about race. We cannot raise our children to think that racism does not exist or not to value and embrace their race as part of their identity. Black Americans will always encounter at least some people who see their race before they see anything else, and we have to prepare our children for those encounters in a way that minimizes the likelihood that they will be traumatized or endangered.

However, we also must avoid rearing kids who see every setback they face through the lens of race and look for opportunities to be offended or outraged. This is what the 1619 Project is in danger of encouraging, and had I continued to embrace such a message in my youth, I never would have graduated from UVA. I personally think it would be more helpful if we could regularly separate the problem of racism—individual and systemic—from the problem of racial inequalities. Eliminating the first, were that possible, would not eliminate the second. That doesn't mean people shouldn't try to be less racist, but they should not deceive themselves to think that in so doing they are saving most black people from anything other than annoyance.

The problems that exist in a portion of the black community will not be solved, or even ameliorated, by a widespread embrace of the 1619 Project. That does not mean that the way we teach American history couldn't be improved. Black Americans—great and ordinary—have achieved incredible things against formidable odds, for themselves and for our country from the time of its founding. The fact that we have been able to embrace the principles of the American Founding, despite the hypocrisy with which those principles were first applied to us, should testify to their power, not justify their weakening or destruction. Freedom and progress require work. And each of us must be willing to pick up our own plows and work until our job is done.

"TRUE FREEDOM COMES FROM SERVING COMMUNITY AND GOD"
BY REV. DEFOREST BLAKE SOARIES JR.

"They shot Dr. King."

That terrible day, of course, was April 4, 1968. I was just a kid, so I didn't know much about Dr. King yet; I just wanted to know why my grandmother was crying.

My parents and I lived with my grandmother until I was in sixth grade. She was a domestic worker, and like so many black women of her generation, she earned very low wages for working long hours. Her husband refused to work, although they had eight children to feed, but somehow, she always had money. And she made the best sweet potato pie in the world.

I knew Dr. King must have been a great man indeed, if learning of his death a thousand miles away could make my grandmother weep like that. And since that day, I have strived to live a life that would mean as much to just one person as Dr. King's life meant to my grandmother.

My quest to follow in Dr. King's footsteps began in the 1970s after the major civil rights demonstrations had ended. I soon discovered that while fighting for freedom could be both dangerous and invigorating, using freedom wisely was an entirely different challenge. By the time

I arrived on the scene, the legislative battles largely had been won. My task—as I saw it—was to motivate people to take advantage of these hard-won opportunities and to resist the temptation to give up.

By the 1980s, I was traveling the entire country, and beyond, still trying to persuade people to embrace the possibilities Dr. King and others died to make available to them. And always, I found myself asking, "What is going on with us? Why aren't we making more progress?"

By the 1990s, I decided to try a different approach. I became the pastor of a little church in the poorest region of central New Jersey. Instead of focusing on the entire nation, I decided to direct my attention to one congregation. Rather than trying to "save the world," I set out to discover what would happen if a local church focused just on loving our neighbors and solving the problems in our community. If we could transform this one little place, we reasoned, then maybe that transformation could spread.

We had plenty of problems to choose from. Crime was high, and our neighborhood's young people were filling the county jail. Drug dealers had the run of countless abandoned buildings, and shootings were so common that we found ourselves picking up bullet shells in the church parking lot almost every Sunday. Despite the country's overall economic growth, unemployment, lack of access to quality health care, and lack of affordable housing made our town an island of poverty in a sea of prosperity. And, perhaps most disturbing of all, there was a surge of pregnant teens checking into hospitals under false names, giving birth, and then abandoning their babies.

My leadership team and I held public meetings and took door-to-door surveys, learning all we could about these problems from the people themselves. We spent eighteen months developing a strategic plan to tackle each one aggressively and methodically. We began by purchasing an abandoned warehouse and—in partnership with St. Peter's Hospital—converted it into a primary care health facility. This facility now treats two thousand patients each week, at least half of whom are uninsured.

Next, we took over a partially completed condominium complex that was being controlled by drug dealers across the street from our church, got rid of the drug dealers, and created affordable homeownership opportunities for community members. Then we convinced a bank that was about to sell its building to a pornography distributer to sell to us instead for one dollar. There, we created a youth center, a community college, and a facility for other neighborhood activities. In response to a special request from the governor, our church also began recruiting families who could take in all those abandoned babies. We started out with about 57 families. Today, we have trained more than 435 families to take in 1,400 children, hundreds of whom have been permanently adopted.

Our church functioned as an economic catalyst and a planning agency for the entire community, and as we had hoped, the transformation has spread. We created a manual for each of our projects, and we still give those manuals to other churches so they can replicate solutions for their own communities. I am extremely grateful that this work has brought hope and renewal to so many. But even in the midst of this success, I still found myself asking the same questions I had two decades earlier: "What is going on with us? Why are we so much less passionate about making use of our freedom than we were about winning it in the first place?"

I found at least part of the answer in the church itself, but not in the way you might expect. During the course of all our community development efforts, our congregation swelled, and we needed a new building. In one sense, this was just another project: we hired an architect, got our permits and loans, and broke ground in 1997. Unlike our community efforts, however, what should have taken eighteen months went on for six years and went $5 million over budget. Suddenly our monthly mortgage payment on the church building was the same as our entire annual budget had been the first year that I pastored.

The church board was understandably unhappy, and I was fully prepared to hand the reins to someone younger who might be able to dig us out of the financial mess. I had been so successful on the community development side that I couldn't fully comprehend how the construction of the church building could get so out of control. But the morning I drove up to the church to resign, the sea of cars in the parking lot caught my eye in a way it hadn't before. For a moment, it was almost as if those Mercedes Benzes, BMWs, Cadillacs, and even a single Maserati were speaking to me.

You could be forgiven for thinking that all those gleaming luxury cars were talking to me about how far we had come as a people. My father was a preacher like me, but he also taught school to pay the bills, and my mother was a secretary. They could never have afforded any of the cars I saw in front of me that morning. But those sedans and coupes weren't congratulating me on how far we had come; they were rebuking me for how far we had fallen because most of their owners couldn't afford them either. Our church project was over budget, but so were far too many of our families.

My parents couldn't have bought a BMW, but they felt no need to buy one either. They paid first and used later, whether it was our house that they saved up for while we were living with my grandmother or a new dress my mother needed that she put on layaway. Like my grandmother, they bought items for functionality and value, and they never used credit for anything. My grandmother herself left real estate to each of her children and her oldest grandchild, while my generation—including many of the owners of those cars—was poised to leave our children nothing but bills.

Things had changed, not just in the black community, but in the nation. Thanks to unprecedented prosperity and a burgeoning advertising industry, we were encouraged to buy products not because they worked well or lasted a long time, but because they would make us feel youthful, attractive, rebellious, or—in the case of an overpriced luxury car—worthy of respect. Staring at those cars in that parking lot, I was forced to confront the possibility that, after working so hard to gain our freedom, at least some of us had just traded one set of oppressors for another.

This is nothing new, of course. Proverbs 22:7 cautioned us thousands of years ago that "the borrower is slave to the lender." That morning revealed our new master to me in all his savagery. And it wasn't the bank who held the car note as much as it was the false promise that material consumption will lead to fulfillment. This lie can be as vicious a master as has ever lived, when coupled with the extension of credit, including by predatory payday lenders whose interest rates the prophets surely would have condemned as usury.

Of course, this master's slaves are hardly confined to the black and the poor. The middle class indulges in "retail therapy," at the cost of their long-term financial freedom. And many of the wealthy have been caught playing fast and loose with credit, but usually with other people's money. Instead of defaulting on a single loan, they bundled countless bad loans together and sent the entire country into a recession.

Programs that focus on financial literacy often neglect both the spiritual and psychological reasons for overspending. Rich, middle-class, and poor alike engage in what I call in my book *Say Yes to No Debt* "compensatory consumption": buying things to compensate for feelings of insignificance. The more we accumulate, the more we want, because our spending never satisfies us the way the master promises it will. Instead it creates overwhelming stress that takes a serious toll on marriages and families. I'd love to say that the American church has stepped up with answers, but unfortunately, one of our fastest-growing segments is full of prosperity preachers who go on television and tell people that God actually wants them to have things they can't afford.

Today, I spend a lot of time trying to free people of all income levels from the self-imposed oppression of compensatory, conspicuous, and confused consumption. I start with a simple and unglamorous principle: There is a difference between what you need and what you want. God will supply all your needs. You have the responsibility to prioritize among your wants because none of us gets to have everything he wants all at once.

After my parking lot epiphany, I knew I had to do more than just get our church budget in the black. I created a special program to help our members free themselves from the new oppressor. Their collective debt burden decreased, and subsequent giving increased to the point where, within a year, our church could easily afford the new mortgage payment (although this was never the goal of the program). To date, our seminars have helped thousands of families control their spending, save and invest for the future, and live debt-free. And they have done so by first reclaiming the liberty that was available to them all along.

The political fight for freedom was difficult and costly; men such as Dr. King paid with their lives. But in the aftermath of that victory, some of us lost the liberty that people like my parents and grandparents had cherished in the midst of legal oppression. My grandmother might not have had the opportunity to go to college or drive to a white-collar job in a Mercedes Benz, but she was freer than many today because she felt no urge to buy stuff she didn't need. She didn't have to get every new dress or pair of shoes she saw to value herself as she went about her day. She was secure and content in who God made her.

When Dr. King led the March on Washington,[117] he wasn't asking for anyone to change the way we felt about ourselves. He was demanding that the laws of the United States of America and the attitudes of its people catch up with what God has said about us from the beginning—that we, like all human beings, are made in His image and likeness and are worthy of equal protection and respect. Only God can give us security and contentedness in who we are. But, in an age of prosperity, that is what defines true freedom.

"HOW HARLEM'S 'HELLFIGHTERS' GAINED THEIR NAME—AND HELPED WIN THE GREAT WAR"

BY STEPHEN L. HARRIS

A t the end of World War I, the 369th United States Infantry Regiment, the all-black National Guard unit composed mostly of citizen-soldiers from New York City, had been in combat longer than any other American regiment—191 days. Their casualties in the Champagne region of France from April 8 to October 1, 1918, were among the highest of any American regiment in the sector. Trained in storefronts and on street corners in New York's borough of Harlem, laughed at and ridiculed, and even perceived as childlike and inferior by the commander of the American Expeditionary Forces, they had never given up a foot of ground in battle.

On the morning of November 17, 1918, six days after the armistice that ended almost five years of war, they marched out of the Vosges Mountains, leading the Allies to the Rhine River, an honor bestowed on them by the respectful French army.

Because of the fierceness of their fighting, these proud doughboys had earned the nickname "Hellfighters," the nom de guerre that defines them still to this day.

Their inspiring story begins in the quarter-century leading up to World War I. For years, Manhattan's African American community had petitioned New York state legislators for a National Guard regiment of its own. Every petition was rebuffed. Then Harlem businessman Charles Fillmore, a veteran of the Spanish-American War, raised a "provisionary" regiment of a thousand citizens. The show of force convinced the state in 1913 to pass legislation establishing New York's first all-black National Guard regiment. Yet the newly enacted law was lost, forgotten, or simply neglected, and for three years no regiment was formed.

But in 1916, when New York's National Guard "Empire" Division, along with divisions and regiments from other states, had been rushed to the Mexican border to protect United States citizens threatened by Pancho Villa and his army that had crossed into New Mexico and murdered seventeen Americans, William Hayward,[118] an aide to New York's governor, discovered the long-lost law that called for a regiment of color. Because the state was literally unprotected with all its National Guard troops two thousand miles away, Hayward, an influential attorney, realized the time was ripe to organize a new regiment—manned by African Americans. Hayward would command the regiment as its colonel.

At last the Fifteenth New York, first known as the "Rattlers," slowly stirred to life. As it turned out, not every able-bodied Harlem male wanted to enlist. One reason was that, throughout the South and Midwest, blacks were being lynched in staggering numbers, and President Woodrow Wilson, a southerner, had yet to speak out against this scourge. Also, a cigar store served as the new regiment's headquarters—hardly an inviting place to draw in potential soldiers. Early recruits trained with broomsticks. Whites derided them as Hayward's "tin soldiers." No wonder filling the ranks of the Fifteenth was a difficult task. Hayward, who thought blacks would join up in droves, was frustrated.

Finding ways to lure men into the regiment posed a problem—until a legend of American jazz showed up. James Reese Europe enlisted in September 1916, wanting to be a gun-toting soldier rather than a musician. At the age of thirty-six, he was among America's foremost composers. In 1912, he conducted the largest African American orchestra yet to play at Carnegie Hall.

With Europe signed up, and along with him, Noble Sissle, another outstanding musician, Hayward sensed he had a golden opportunity to swell the ranks of his regiment by creating a military band like no other, a band with a ragtime jazz beat. So, in December 1916, to get the kind of band he envisioned, Hayward turned to his famous recruit.

Advertisements soon appeared in African American newspapers, offering "An Opportunity for Musicians—Crack Colored Musicians." It wasn't long before Hayward had a seventy-five-member band, almost twice the regulation size of other regimental bands. Performing on the streets of Harlem, its jazz music did more for recruiting than Hayward had hoped and, within weeks—and with America on the verge of war with Germany—the Fifteenth reached full regimental strength of 2,002 men and fifty-six officers, making it the country's first National Guard regiment to hit wartime strength.

After the United States declared war on Germany, it had to furiously build up its military strength. Guard units soon bulged with men. Among the first of the citizen-soldier regiments to head for France was the Fifteenth. Before it sailed, however, it had to deal with racists at Camp Wadsworth in Spartanburg, South Carolina.

Obviously, the United States War Department used poor judgment when it ordered the Fifteenth to South Carolina to train. The order came soon after whites in East St. Louis slaughtered more than one hundred blacks.[119] Southerners feared Yankees of color and threatened to harm them. Hayward's men swore that if they were menaced or beaten up, they would not raise a hand in retaliation. They endured taunts. They were thrown off sidewalks. After less than two weeks at Camp Wadsworth, the Fifteenth was sent back to New York. The moment a troopship became available, the regiment was off to France.

On the way over, Noble Sissle brooded: "We were the Baby National Guard Regiment of New York, had no armory, no previous military experience—just a bunch of much-made-over boys under the leadership of a politician colonel. Before any of us were aware of it, we found ourselves in the middle of the Atlantic Ocean, going to fight. Only half-equipped and no training in modern warfare—not even a part of any division. Just a single little regiment. Even the colonel did not know what we were going to do after we got to France."

If Hayward and his men thought they'd be ordered to the Western Front, they were sorely disappointed. Instead of rifles, the regiment received picks and shovels and was assigned to perform common labor at the port of St. Nazaire. The colonel kept bombarding Gen. John J. Pershing for inclusion in the American Expeditionary Forces, but Pershing ignored his pleas. Hayward fumed. He called his troops orphans, claiming, "My regiment was left by Gen. Pershing on the doorstep of France."

Meanwhile, James Reese Europe and his handpicked musicians brought jazz to France in a big way. In mid-February 1918, the Young Men's Christian Association (YMCA) opened the first leave area for American soldiers in the famous resort village of Aix-les-Bains in the French Alps. One of its top acts was to be the Fifteenth Regimental Band. To get there from the coast, the band traveled by train. It stopped at villages along the way and performed concerts in village squares and parks, introducing jazz throughout most of France.

When the musicians arrived at Aix-les-Bains, canteen worker Marian Baldwin wrote in her diary, "They are perfectly screaming, but a marvelous band, and when they came marching down the streets to meet the troops yesterday, the French people went perfectly wild over them."

At Aix-les-Bains, the band was so popular it stayed for a month. At its last concert, doughboys went wild, waving flags in support of their African American comrades in arms. "On stage," wrote an officer of the Fifteenth, "the colored soldiers who had been spat upon in Spartanburg, South Carolina, rose and bowed—and grinned."

While Europe, Sissle, and the band had been wowing doughboys and French civilians alike in the Alps, Hayward, at last, got the orders he wanted. His regiment was to be posted to the front lines—but not with the American Expeditionary Forces. The Fifteenth New York was redesignated the 369th United States Infantry Regiment, as part of the newly organized all-black 93rd Infantry Division,[120] a division on paper only, and attached to the Sixteenth Division of the French Fourth Army, commanded by the one-armed Gen. Henri Gouraud.

By mid-April, the Hellfighters were in the Champagne sector northeast of Châlons, protecting a swath of the west bank of the Aisne River. It marked the first time black American soldiers had entered the front line in the Great War.

On the night of May 13, Henry Johnson, a pint-sized redcap from Albany, New York, hunkered down in a listening post out in no man's land. He shared the mudhole with Pvt. Needham Roberts from Trenton, New Jersey. Out of the darkness, pitching grenades and firing rifles, a German platoon, attacked the two soldiers. Both Americans fell. Johnson suffered three gunshot wounds, but he struggled to his feet and singlehandedly met the rush. Using a bolo knife, he repelled the assault, certainly killing a half dozen men. His fury forced the Germans to retreat. For his heroic stand, Johnson received France's award for valor, the Croix de Guerre. Newspapers throughout the United States carried his story.

Because one of America's first war heroes was a soldier of color, the black community renewed its efforts to convince President Wilson to repudiate lynching. Finally, Wilson publicly stated that anyone taking part in a mob action is "no true son of this great democracy, but its betrayer."[121]

(In 2015, the U.S. government posthumously awarded the country's highest award for valor, the Congressional Medal of Honor, to Henry Johnson.[122])

The 369th was just getting warmed up. Transferred to the 161st French Division, the New Yorkers relieved a Moroccan battalion. In mid-July, they bravely helped repulse a massive German attack in the Second Battle of the Marne. By stopping the enemy, the Hellfighters, along with other American soldiers and French soldiers, turned the tide of the Great War. For the next two months, they took part in the drive by the Allies that forced the German Army to retreat to the Hindenburg Line.

Then, starting on September 26, British, Belgian, French, and American armies began their all-out strike against the Germans. On that day, the valiant men of the 369th pushed forward under heavy fire. They stormed the heights of Bellevue Ridge, to the village of Ripont, crossed the Dormois River—turning it red with their own blood—and then battled to the outskirts of Sechault, a strongly fortified town that French Gen. Henri Pétain swore could not be taken. The attack proved costly, yet the New Yorkers—in fierce street-to-street fighting—drove out the enemy and captured Sechault.

For its gallantry, the entire regiment received not only the Croix de Guerre from the French government but also the honorific "Hellfighters." The citation reads, in part: "Though engaging in an offensive for the first time, [the 369th Regiment] fought with great bravery, stormed powerful enemy positions energetically defended, captured many machine guns, large numbers of prisoners and six cannon and took, after heavy fighting, the Town of Sechault." The taking of Sechault ended the 369th's major combat operations.

On February 17, 1919, the 369th returned home to a tumultuous parade up Manhattan's famed Fifth Avenue and then through the streets of Harlem. On crowded sidewalks, cheering New Yorkers embraced their newest heroes. In the years and decades that followed, the Hellfighters served during World War II, Korea, Vietnam, and Desert Storm. The Empire State had its black National Guard Regiment, and these men of color were orphans no more.

"A DREAM AS OLD AS THE AMERICAN DREAM: WHY BLACK PATRIOTISM IS MORE IMPORTANT THAN VICTIMIZATION"
BY CLARENCE PAGE

In 2019, marking four hundred years since the first known Africans arrived on these shores from West Africa as slaves, the *New York Times* launched its ambitious 1619 Project. It aims to reexamine U.S. history through the lens of black history—as if American history began with the arrival of the first black folks. The concept was well intended, and the execution of its first episode well documented. Yet it left me feeling that the *Times* missed at least half of the story. By looking through the lens of black victimization, it paid too little attention to what I call "black overcoming"—our victories over adversity and achievements of success, sometimes in conflict but also often in cooperation with people from other races and ethnic groups.

The *Times* incorrectly assumes that the challenges facing particularly inner-city blacks are related to a legacy of slavery and discrimination. This is patently untrue. Let's look at the issue of poverty and how we're treated.

Our perceptions are distorted by the "colorization of poverty" in the mid-1960s. Media images of President Johnson's "War on

Poverty" focused mostly on poor whites in Appalachia,[123] where LBJ announced his initiative—and where I later would work with mostly white teens in the Upward Bound program as a college student in 1967. But with the outbreak of riots in Watts, Harlem, Chicago, and other urban centers, news media images of rural poverty were replaced by images from the "ghetto."

Colorization has had a profound impact on other issues too. In the 1980s, for example, crack cocaine was perceived as a mostly black problem and a law enforcement issue. In the 1990s, opioid addiction was perceived as a mostly rural white problem and a public health issue.

J. D. Vance, writing in *Hillbilly Elegy* about growing up in the same Ohio town where I grew up almost two generations earlier, ignited a new discussion from the grassroots of white poverty and drugs that showed me the important similarities between poor blacks and whites in America, despite the tribalism encouraged by demagogic leaders of both races. "I have known many welfare queens," Vance writes. "Some were my neighbors, and all were white." His candor is refreshing.[124]

Vance tends to view poverty in the way many people in the traditionally Republican town of Middletown, Ohio, view it: as a problem of culture, morality, character, and personal responsibility. I agree that personal character matters, but I also have witnessed those values undermined by what William Julius Wilson called "the disappearance of work,"[125] Ohio's well-paying, low-skill industrial jobs that lured Vance's family from Kentucky and mine from Alabama.

Vance's book forced me to take a new look at my life and hometown, and at our similarities and our differences. Vance explains in his introduction how personal stories offer cultural insights that are essential to any serious discussion of equal opportunity: "Nobel-winning economists worry about the decline of the industrial Midwest and the hollowing out of the economic core of working whites," he writes. "What they mean is that manufacturing jobs have gone overseas and middle-class jobs are harder to come by for people without college degrees. Fair enough—I worry about those things, too. But this book is about something else: what goes on in the lives of real people when the industrial economy goes south. It's about reacting to bad circumstances in the worst way possible. It's about a culture that increasingly encourages social decay instead of counteracting it."

It's not laziness that's destroying hillbilly culture, says Vance. It's what psychologist Martin Seligman calls "learned helplessness."[126] Too many of us African Americans have picked up that malady too.

Where should we go from here? Similarities between Vance's life and mine showed me how much we Americans need to desegregate our poverty discussion to learn across the lines of race and class the true causes of poverty and inequality—and, more importantly, what works to solve them.

Yes, blacks have fought to make true the ideals in our nation's founding documents, as the *New York Times* says. But its statement that the "founding ideals were false" is misleading, and even counterproductive to our understanding of the founding documents as aspirational. The principle that "all men," or people, "are created equal" was true in early American law only for white, property-owning men, but the Founders, as a minority themselves, wisely took that principle of equality very seriously in the abstract, understanding they themselves might need it someday. They established a tradition: guarantee "inalienable rights" to some but also establish the legal mechanisms to extend those equal protections to others without—and this is important—taking those rights away from those who have them.

Our 1776 Unites project puts less of an emphasis on history and more on the question prophetically raised by the Rev. Martin Luther King Jr. at the height of his civil rights revolution: "Where do we go from here?"[127] Mindful of the inevitable critics' charge that his movement was subversive, King made a special effort to ground his historic 1963 "I Have a Dream" speech in "a dream as old as the American dream"[128] by repeated references to the nation's founding documents, including Abraham Lincoln's Gettysburg Address. He assured friends and foes alike that his civil rights movement had come not to deny the gospel of the American Dream but to fulfill it.

We must disrupt the long-held stereotypes of black people as helpless bystanders in their own history. We have had entrepreneurs, skilled tradesmen, military officers, inventors, organizers, and many others who responded to adversity by marshaling resources, building local enterprises, and creating jobs. We organized and acted to defeat slavery, segregation, and deprivation, and then we persevered to build businesses that included banks, hotels, small factories, and a black-owned railroad.

In addition to the consequences of slavery, these contributions of black Americans should be at the very center of the story we tell ourselves about who we are. Even in bondage, slaves had agency in various amounts, or to varying degrees, and they acted on it in a variety of ways. Those who prefer to focus on our victimization don't always want to recognize it, but the ways our ancestors exercised agency in bondage formed the foundation of their successes (or failures) after they were freed.

Americans are optimistic people, but we care more about the future than the past. We care about the past mostly as much as it helps us to deal with the uncertainties of our future. Changes, demographic and otherwise, are tearing us apart. Our historic victimization must never be forgotten, but it is best remembered though the stories of our groundbreaking victories over oppression through faith, courage, talent, persistence, ingenuity, and hard work.

It may be a cliché these days to note that our differences should not be allowed to stand in the way of what we share in common, but too often they still do. We must find ways to appreciate the contributions that our diverse population makes to American life. We need to study not only the atrocities of U.S. history but also America's magnificent capacity for self-improvement as we seek the tools and knowledge to help us face our shared future with new hope—together.

"CHILDREN ACHIEVE THE EXPECTATIONS WE TEACH: CHARTING A PATH TO A MORE PERFECT UNION BEGINS WITH OUR GUIDANCE"

BY IAN ROWE

> *"We the people, in order to form a more perfect union ...'—221 years ago, in a hall that still stands across the street, a group of men gathered and, with these simple words, launched America's improbable experiment in democracy."*
>
> —Barack Obama

On March 18, 2008, then-presidential candidate Obama thus began an oratory that Andrew Sullivan at the *Atlantic* called a "searing, nuanced, gut-wrenching, loyal, and deeply, deeply Christian speech" and "the most honest speech on race in America in my adult lifetime."[129] Standing in the Constitution Center in Philadelphia, Obama argued that despite America's original sin of the abomination of slavery, he was optimistic that future generations would continue to make progress towards "a more perfect union," precisely because our nation was founded on the principles ratified in the Constitution of 1789, when "America's improbable experiment in democracy" was launched.[130]

Recalling Obama's speech is relevant amidst today's fierce debate as to what to teach young Americans about the nation's origin story and true birthdate. Like Obama, some posit that it is 1789, the year the Constitution went into effect, establishing the American form of government. Most Americans believe it was 1776, upon the signing of the Declaration of Independence and the enumeration of the unalienable rights of life, liberty, and the pursuit of happiness. Some historians say it is technically 1507, when a map known as "America's Birth Certificate"[131] was the first to depict the name "America," a Latinized version of "Amerigo" Vespucci, the Italian explorer who was the first person to recognize the lands to which Christopher Columbus sailed in 1492 were part of a separate continent. "America" is identified in the top portion of this segment of a map created in 1507 by Martin Waldseemüller.[132]

Against this backdrop enters the 1619 Project, an initiative from the *New York Times* that commemorates "the 400th anniversary of the beginning of American slavery, and aims to reframe the country's history by placing the consequences of slavery and the contributions of black Americans at the very center of our national narrative."

In addition to convincing *Times Magazine* readers that "our democracy's founding ideals were false when they were written,"[133] the 1619 Project is making a concerted effort to ensure the next generation develops a warped view of America as well. Random House Group has acquired the rights to the 1619 Project and will develop a graphic novel and series of four publications for young people. The Pulitzer Center has become the project's education partner. According to its annual report,[134] the Pulitzer Center has provided free reading guides, extension activities, lesson plans, and physical copies of the magazine to hundreds of schools and teachers across all fifty states, who have brought curricular resources to some 3,500 classrooms.

Indeed, some of the poorest school districts in the country, with the lowest performance levels in reading and math, have adopted the 1619 Project as mandatory curriculum for their high school students. In cities such as Chicago, Newark, and Buffalo, with high concentrations of minority students, what will these young minds now be learning?

Central to the thesis of 1619 is that this nation was founded not as a democracy but as a slavocracy; that white racist supremacy is irrevocably intertwined in the country's DNA; that plantation slave-labor camps were the catalyst for an enduring system of brutal American capitalism;[135] and as Nikole Hannah-Jones, the person who spearheaded the 1619 Project, asserted, it is "time for this country to pay what is owed." She explains that reparations—in the form of cash payments—would be due to anyone who can "trace a descendant back to American slavery," and who can "prove that 10 years prior to the discussion of the reparations bill, you actually lived as a black person."[136]

Since 2010, I have run a network of public charter schools that now educates more than two thousand predominantly black and Hispanic students in the heart of low-income communities in the South Bronx and Lower East Side of Manhattan. Because of frustration with their zoned schools, parents must enter a random lottery to gain entry to our open-enrollment schools. While parents themselves have faced structural barriers around race, and fear that their children will as well, they know a great education can make the difference. They do not believe that their children are doomed to be shackled by the horrors of America's legacy of slavery. On the contrary, they want our teachers to provide the kind of quality education that equips their kids with the skills, knowledge, and habits of mind to thrive in America.

That is what is so disturbing and dangerous about the 1619 Project's aspiration for children: to create in the minds of students and teachers of all races a vision of America that is imbued with a permanent malignancy that is hostile to the dreams of students of color.

It is simply wrong.

As educators, we must reject these tired ideas that lead to the soft bigotry of low expectations. We do our scholars no favors by treating them as victims because of a group identity, or by teaching them to become dependent on a government system, such as reparations, in order to succeed in their own lives. As Burgess Owens writes in the *Wall Street Journal*, "At the core of the reparation movement is a divisive and demeaning view of both races. It grants to the white race a wicked superiority, treating them as an oppressive people too powerful for black Americans to overcome. It brands blacks as hapless victims devoid of the ability, which every other culture possesses, to assimilate and progress. Neither label is earned."[137]

Black students growing up in low-income communities are inundated with messages from many adults in their lives that they will be preyed upon because of their race. Rather than reinforce this false idea of powerlessness in the face of a system rigged against them, why not educate young people of color about the forces within their control that are most likely to put them on a pathway to power and economic success?

For example, in 2014, a team of researchers led by Harvard's Raj Chetty investigated the intergenerational mobility of more than forty million children and their parents. What factors led to certain communities having high rates of economic mobility across generations, and others in which few children escape poverty? The "Land of Opportunity" study they produced found that "the strongest predictors of upward mobility are measures of family structure such as the fraction of single parents in the area."[138]

A growing body of research underscores the transcendent role that individual decisions about the timing of family formation can play in achieving the American Dream. Indeed, a staggering 97 percent of millennials who followed the "success sequence"—getting at least a high school degree, working full-time, and marrying before having any children, in that order—avoided poverty.[139] And "Black Men, Making It in America: The Engines of Economic Success for Black Men in America," reveals that a number of factors—education, work, marriage, church participation, military service, and a sense of personal agency[140]—are all highly correlated to black male economic success in America.

Shouldn't our young people be taught to understand the pathways more likely to have them flourish financially, rather than perpetuate the noxious notion that black kids are owed something and that their path to success must be paved by a massive government handout?

It is ironic that Nikole Hannah-Jones herself exemplifies how sticking to this middle-class script in her own life is creating opportunity for her children. In the autobiographic *New York Times* story "Choosing a School for My Daughter in a Segregated City,"[141] and in discussion about busing and desegregation, Hannah-Jones courageously shares the fears that she and her husband had about enrolling four-year-old Najya in a segregated, low-income school in Brooklyn. After describing all of the machinations that went into their decision, Hannah-Jones makes a revealing statement: "I also knew that we would be able to make up for Najya anything the school was lacking."[142] Consider the confidence and privilege Hannah-Jones expressed in her and her husband's ability to ensure their daughter succeeds. No amount of anti-black racism, or putting their daughter in a high-poverty, all-black school, could overcome the power of the stable, two-parent home she and her husband provide.

Ultimately, I know that the black and brown children from the schools I lead are entering a world in which factors related to race, class, or gender will force them to confront extraordinary challenges while simultaneously being exposed to extraordinary opportunities. The question is, what will make the difference in whether these young scholars succumb to challenge or thrive on opportunity, whether they develop a mindset of enslavement or empowerment?

We cannot deprive young black children—or kids of all races—of the knowledge of the series of decisions that Nikole Hannah-Jones, millions of black Americans, and I have pursued on our pathway to economic prosperity and achievement of the American Dream.

Many of us in the black community must preach what we have practiced in order to achieve our own levels of professional success—and more importantly, share what we are teaching our children to help them have the greatest likelihood to achieve their chosen path of fulfillment. For many of us, this goes well beyond just having "The Talk" with our black sons about avoiding police brutality.

It also means communicating to our sons and daughters that they have power in their individual choices, and that those decisions can shape their destiny despite structural barriers associated with race, class, and poverty.

As the 1619 Project correctly points out, America's tortured history will forever be scarred by the horrific stories of chattel enslavement. But where are the empowering stories of progress? What the project completely misses is the peculiar duality of America. As Hendrik Hertzberg and Henry Louis Gates Jr. wrote in the 1996 *New Yorker* special edition, Black in America, "For African-Americans, the country of oppression and the country of liberation are the same country."[143]

In closing his 2008 speech on race, Obama described the path towards a more perfect union:

> For the African American community, that path means embracing the burdens of our past without becoming victims of our past. It means continuing to insist on a full measure of justice in every aspect of American life. But it also

means binding our particular grievances—for better health care and better schools and better jobs—to the larger aspirations of all Americans: the white woman struggling to break the glass ceiling, the white man who has been laid off, the immigrant trying to feed his family. And it means taking full responsibility for our own lives—by demanding more from our fathers, and spending more time with our children, and reading to them, and teaching them that while they may face challenges and discrimination in their own lives, they must never succumb to despair or cynicism; they must always believe that they can write their own destiny.[144]

Regardless of where the pushpin falls on America's timeline of discovery, what really matters is its future and the power of black—and all—Americans to shape this shared destiny.

"FROM RURAL POVERTY TO IVY LEAGUE PROFESSOR: CAROL M. SWAIN'S LIFE LESSONS"
BY CAROL M. SWAIN

As a black American who grew up in the rural South in the 1950s, I have witnessed firsthand systemic racism and the tremendous progress we have made in America in terms of race relations and opportunities.

I lived in the country woods of southwestern Virginia, in a family that eventually included twelve children. I was the second oldest. My earliest childhood memories include living in a tar paper-covered, two-room shack without indoor plumbing or running water. The shack had a tin roof, wood cooking stove, and walls without insulation. And for a few years, the children slept on the kitchen floor.

The poverty I experienced meant that water for bathing each morning had to be heated on the stove and shared with others. Water for cooking, bathing, and cleaning came from a spring located downhill from a cemetery. We lacked proper clothes and adequate food. Whenever the snow was deep, my siblings and I stayed home from school until it melted. Once we missed 80 of 180 school days, and my siblings and I failed.

Eventually, we each reached the eighth grade and dropped out of school. I dropped out in the ninth grade, married at sixteen, had my first child at seventeen, and by the age of twenty, I had three small children. This could have defined my life. I could have stayed on welfare after my divorce and repeated the cycle of poverty. After all, I had witnessed real systemic racism.

But I had a mother who was too proud for her children to accept free lunches or free schoolbooks. Despite our poverty, my mother never spoke about racism or about societal limitations. We all believed only rich people could go to college. Early marriage and starting a family seemed desirable.

I was hopeless and trapped. But people entered my life who encouraged me by telling me I was intelligent, and I could do more with my life. These people included an African orderly from Sierra Leone and a twenty-five-year-old doctor completing his residency at a local hospital. Many of my mentors and encouragers have been white men and women. These became role models.

Despite the poverty, I believed I could make good things happen and that I was not destined to remain poor. Eventually, I divorced, earned a high school equivalency, and entered a community college, where I earned the first of five college and university degrees.

A brief stint on welfare convinced me I needed to get an education so I could get a "good" job. It never occurred to me as I was studying, working, and rearing my children that the world was stacked against me or that it owed me a better break because of my race, impoverished roots, female gender, or family status. I believed I could achieve the American Dream, and I did.

It would take graduate school and studies of oppression to reveal to me that people from my background were "doomed to poverty" because of oppression and systemic racism. Fortunately, I was successful and thriving before I heard these depressing messages.

My belief in the American Dream and its possibilities inspired me to aim high. I made the dean's list at Virginia Western Community College and graduated magna cum laude from Roanoke College while working forty hours a week, nights and weekends, at Virginia Western, where I earned my first degree. As a senior at Roanoke

College I spearheaded the establishment of the Constance J. Hamlar Scholarship for minorities. Today, it is an endowed fund that has helped support hundreds of minorities.

Although I was not a declared conservative, I have always had conservative values. I was determined to be married before I had children. I believed and still believe in America and the promise it offers people of every race and ethnicity.

Ingrained in me was not hatred or bitterness. I was optimistic about the future, despite periods of despair. My civic education instilled in me a strong appreciation for America and the state of Virginia, the home of U.S. presidents and of Booker T. Washington, a former slave and founder of the Tuskegee Institute. His autobiography, *Up from Slavery*, continues to inspire me and anyone who takes the time to read it.

There is hope for America. As a strong individualist, I reject groupthink and question the behaviors and thought patterns of those who complain about systemic racism as being a limiting factor for blacks. It is the internalization of the false narrative that the world is stacked against blacks and that nothing has changed much that limits possibilities and keeps people trapped in cycles of poverty and hopelessness.

Here are some life lessons I learned from my journey from rural poverty to success as a tenured professor at Vanderbilt and Princeton universities, and now as a public intellectual:

- Everyone has the potential to overcome life's disadvantages.
- Where you start your life does not determine where you end up.
- Your attitude toward life, and what you believe about reality, are far more important than your race, gender, or social class in determining what you will accomplish in life.
- Everyone is unique and special. If you do your part with what you have been given, God will do the rest.

Because I learned these lessons and tried to hold on to them, I did not let being black, female, and being born into an underprivileged family become stumbling blocks. None of these so-called societal disadvantages became a crippling factor for me. What has been more challenging for me than the alleged systemic racism we hear about daily is the discrimination people who think like me face in the world of academia and the mainstream media because we dare to be different. Indeed, we march to the tune of a different drummer.

"CLOSING THE BLACK-WHITE EDUCATIONAL GAP IN THE SOUTH IN THE EARLY TWENTIETH CENTURY"

BY STEPHANIE DEUTSCH

Shortly after the publication of my book, *You Need a Schoolhouse: Booker T. Washington, Julius Rosenwald, and the Building of Schools for the Segregated South*, an interviewer asked me, "What was your big takeaway from the research you did?" I had never asked myself quite that question, but it didn't take me long to find the answer: respect for African Americans. The result of my research into the circumstances surrounding the building of schools for African American children in the early decades of the twentieth century was, for me, a newfound respect and admiration for the people who, despite the enslavement of their ancestors and the harsh reality of their present circumstances, did not lose faith in their country in troubled, turbulent, often desperately discouraging times.

Like generations of Americans before and after them, they placed great hope for the future in education. In the face of economic uncertainty, frequent violence, and relentless prejudice, they were willing to make sacrifices to ensure that their children had schools to go to. The 4,977 Rosenwald schools[145] for African American children built across the South between 1913 and 1932 were the result of a remarkable three-way public-private partnership conceived by Booker T. Washington—money provided by public school systems; grants from Julius Rosenwald, the wealthy president of Sears, Roebuck and Company; and contributions from local communities, predominantly from African American men and women who, dollar for dollar, contributed more to the creation of the schools than their wealthy benefactor. By the early 1950s, one-third of the African American children in the South were being educated in Rosenwald schools.

It was serendipity for me that my book came out just as a movement was gaining steam to preserve many of these simple, mostly wooden structures, which, once segregation ended, usually were discarded as no longer needed. A few continued as schools; some passed into private hands and became houses or barns; others were torn down. Many were in such remote locations that no one quite knew what happened to them. In 2002, the National Trust for Historic Preservation named the Rosenwald schools to its annual list of most endangered historic sites in the nation. Proud alumni of the schools had begun an effort, ongoing today, to preserve these schoolhouses and, more importantly, the legacy they represent—a legacy I have experienced when meeting scores of men and women who attended the schools. Their pride in the forebears whose vision and generosity provided the schools, and in the way they themselves benefited from the education they received there, filled me with admiration.

When I began the research for my book, I had thought I was well informed. I, of course, knew something about slavery and the agony of the Civil War. I had lived through the tumultuous days of challenge and change in the late 1950s and '60s. But it turned out there was a significant blank space in my knowledge—the hundred years between Abraham Lincoln's eloquent call to generosity of spirit and Martin Luther King Jr.'s dream. After the Thirteenth and Fourteenth Amendments and Reconstruction came laws restricting, rather than expanding, opportunity for African Americans—*Plessy v. Ferguson* enshrining "separate but equal" in law, for example, and states rewriting their constitutions to make it more difficult for blacks and others to exercise the right to vote—along with an extra-legal system of social control, lynching.

In theory, I knew about these things, but in fact, I had not understood what they meant. I had thought of prejudice as a feeling. I had no concept of Jim Crow—prejudice enshrined in an ever-expanding body of law, one imitated by the Nazis in the 1930s as they restricted life for Jews. I thought of lynching as a very occasional horror, not the gruesome deaths of thousands of individuals over a fifty-year span, a spectacle sometimes applauded by white mobs that included children. The shame and horror I felt as I learned this history deepened my growing regard for the men and women I was meeting at Rosenwald school events.

I heard from many different people stories about walking to school—sometimes a mile or two or three—and being passed by school buses carrying white children to their schools. Sometimes the white children laughed or made faces at them. Once, on a sparkling fall day in Virginia, I heard about this from a group of Rosenwald alumnae as we walked down a country road, past a house flying a Confederate flag. They told me about their textbooks, cast-offs from white schools, used and soiled and sometimes with nasty messages scrawled inside. But I also heard about the devoted teachers who often boarded with local families and offered children steady encouragement with the admonition to "go out and be a credit to your race." I was told about "soup day," when one parent would bring lunch for everyone, about spelling bees and dances around the Maypole, and the annual recitation of the Gettysburg Address.

Watching documentary footage of women and men walking to work, which they did for almost a year in Montgomery, Alabama, during the bus boycott of 1955, I realized that many of them or their parents or their aunts and uncles no doubt had been educated in Rosenwald schools. They had learned not just spelling and count-ing, but embracing a sense of citizenship. The portraits of Abraham Lincoln and Booker T. Washington that looked down from the bead-board walls around them, and the American flags in the corners of their classrooms, were part of the lessons they absorbed.

In a long-shuttered school in the Northern Neck of Virginia I put my hand in a dusty box and pulled out a civics textbook from 1920. I opened it and read, "The purpose of the public school is to prepare students to be good citizens." Learning about a student walkout at a North Carolina Rosenwald high school that was to be closed because of integration, I began to understand the loss experienced in the black community as the country lurched from mandated separation to enforced integration. In the face of exclusion and hostility, African Americans had built up magnificent institutions—schools, colleges, businesses, churches, sororities. Not all of these would survive. There would be loss and pain, as well as the thrill of progress, in the transi-tion to a hoped-for more perfect union.

Like the men and women who contributed to building Rosenwald schools, I believe in the power of education. To understand the pres-ent, it is crucial to know what has gone before, not just in order to right the wrongs but to build on the strengths. My own understanding of the present has been immeasurably enriched by deepening my appre-ciation for what has gone before. Our present is the result of a painful evolution from our founding, with its tacit acceptance of the fact that the newly established United States was being built on an impossible contradiction—the assertion that "all men are created equal" while one portion of the population enslaved another—through the gruesome physical fight to end slavery and then the struggle to more closely align reality to our majestic national principles.

This road certainly has been stony. Every American needs to know that and feel something of that pain. But that evolution also has been guided by faith in the rule of law, by respect for our founding principles, by optimism, and by powerful voices of reason.

Among those, no voice was more eloquent than that of Frederick Douglass. In his brilliant new biography, historian David Blight[146] charts Douglass's growth over a long career from an abolitionist fueled by fury and outrage to one whose confidence in the future was built on knowledge of and love for, among other things, the Declaration of Independence. "The forces against us," Douglass said in one of his many speeches, "are passion and prejudice, which are transient, and those for us are principles, self-acting, self-sustaining and permanent."

The principle that all people are created equal, and the notion that they are endowed by their creator with the "unalienable" rights to life, liberty, and the pursuit of happiness, could not possibly mean more to anyone than to those who, like Douglass, experienced the hideous indignities of slavery. All Americans owe a debt of gratitude not just to the Founders who, in 1776, so powerfully articulated these magnificent principles, but also to the generations since who have never lost faith in them.

"AN ALGORITHM OF SUCCESS: UNDERSTANDING BLACK AMERICA"

BY JOHN SIBLEY BUTLER

D ecades ago, I arrived at the National Center for Neighborhood Enterprise to chat with Robert L. Woodson Sr. and William Raspberry, the late outstanding columnist for the *Washington Post*, about research on the success paradigm of black Americans. After presenting the manuscript, Raspberry noted, "You had better put all of the data in the book because people will never believe your paradigm."

In 1977, the first edition of *Entrepreneurship and Self-Help among Black Americans: A Reconsideration of Race and Economics* was published. Relying on scholarship that lay dormant for years, the book explains how black Americans created a blueprint for success for future generations. Data for the work were taken from scholars who documented the success of black Americans under difficult circumstances. These works include W. E. B. DuBois's *Economic Co-Operation among Negro Americans* (1898) and *The College-Bred Negro American* (1911); Abram L. Harris's *The Negro as Capitalist* (1918); Booker T. Washington's *The Negro in Business* (1906); Charles Johnson's *Negro College Graduate* (1947); and Joseph A. Pierce's *Negro Business and Business Education* (1947).

My book allows comparisons between other groups of all races who follow this paradigm; among variables that are important, especially the relationship between entrepreneurship and education of children, there are striking similarities. Understanding the success model of America means understanding differences between segregation, homophily, and different modes of adjustment to America, one of the greatest market economies that has ever existed. We have over 150 years of data to help us understand strategies that lead to success in America under all kinds of circumstances.

So what is it that leads to success?

If we were to create a learning algorithm for group success, and indeed non-success, through the generations, we would start with how groups enter market economies, either with an emphasis on wage labor or as entrepreneurs. The algorithm would tell us that, in the aggregate, those groups that entered by putting self-employment at their very centers, and also created educational structures for success, have much better outcomes than those who joined the workforce as laborers without creating institutional structures. In a real sense, America is the story of how different racial and religious groups (and combinations of both) come together and place entrepreneurship at the center of community. When this is done voluntarily, sociologists call it "homophily," often defined as "birds of a feather flock together."

As noted by Max Weber in *The Protestant Ethic and the Spirit of Capitalism,* when there is discrimination and no opportunities to serve the state, groups are driven into economic entrepreneurship and become very successful.[147] One can think of white Jews in Europe, the Igbo in Africa, Mormons in America, and the Japanese in California. Future generations among these groups have an intense interest in entrepreneurship and education. Segments of black America throughout history also fall into this equation, because during the days of forced segregation, no group carried out the algorithm better. Under segregation, there was an intense homophily that placed entrepreneurship and education at the center of community.

The effects of putting entrepreneurship and institution-building at the center of community began to appear in Henry M. Minton's 1911 work, *Early History of Negroes in Business in Philadelphia.* The impact of self-employment was significant because entrepreneurs served as leaders of the community. This effect was further synthesized in Dubois's *The College-Bred Negro American.* By 1938, Johnson's *Negro College Graduate* was able to show that blacks in the entrepreneurial tradition were in their third generation of college matriculation.

Decades of research into the failure of blacks has obscured this relationship between self-employment and education. As a result, the country is reluctant to understand this groundbreaking blueprint established by early black Americans. Recently, the chancellor of my undergraduate institution informed me that he is proud that the institution would be graduating "first-generation college graduates," using code for black Americans. I answered by noting that when I enrolled in Louisiana State University in 1965, most incoming black students were second- and third-generation college graduates. Before there was desegregation, there was a strong tradition of black college graduates because of the entrepreneurial spirit of parents, grandparents, and great-grandparents.

How strong was this entrepreneurial tradition? Margaret Levenstein's 2004 research, *African American Entrepreneurship: The View from the 1910 Census,* shows that black Americans were more likely than white Americans to be employers, and almost as likely as whites to be self-employed. This was the result of free blacks setting the standard prior to the Civil War and Booker T. Washington and his Tuskegee Machine, which took self-employment of blacks to a different level under his National Negro Business League.[148] While in a constant battle with the NAACP, which was founded to blunt the effects of his Tuskegee Machine, black Americans created communities that produced entrepreneurs who supported private black colleges—some established with the help of northern black merchants after the Civil War and the majority established by black religious institutions—and universities and continued the success of the group.

In recent years, more scholars have captured this buried history. Robert Kenzer's *Enterprising Southerners* (1997); Margo Jefferson's *Negroland* (2016); Elizabeth Dowling Taylor's *The Original Black Elite* (2018); and *Black Georgetown Remembered* (1991) by Kathleen Lesko, Valerie Babb, and Carroll Gibbs all are in this tradition. There also is renewed interest in scholarship that documents the emergence of black wealth under entrepreneurship. These include *Black Fortunes* by Shomari Wills; *Staking a Claim: Jake Simmons, Jr. and the Making of an Oil Dynasty* by Jonathan Greenberg; and popular magazines such as *Fortune,* which documents the evolution of black millionaires.

To be sure, not all black Americans followed this model of entrepreneurship and self-help. Like many other Americans, they followed the model that stressed the importance of wage labor and the presence of factories. Both models are acceptable but produce different results. When factories fail, the results are devastating. This can be seen in William Julius Wilson's book, *The Declining Significance of Race.* Using Chicago as a laboratory, Wilson showed how communities became "hoods" and crime increased as industries failed that city. A similar pattern was seen all over the industrial North and affected all people. But many blacks, who embraced education and entrepreneurship, did not experience such fates.

Wilson's work is in the tradition of what I have termed the "failure paradigm"; there is no place for self-employment in that model. Indeed, there was no need to emphasize education because factory jobs do not require education. One could complete high school, during the glory days of the North, join a union, and have an outstanding work experience. But when homophily—that is, self-sustaining ecosystems of educated black entrepreneurs—was applied under segregation, the effects were substantial. Thus, by 1992, when work had disappeared in the North, states that led in the percentage of black college graduates were Mississippi, Louisiana, Georgia, South Carolina, and Alabama. These are all southern states with strong histories of legal segregation, but high levels of entrepreneurship and self-help among black Americans.

The failure paradigm, which neglects the blueprint of success, has influenced commentary on black Americans. Indeed, E. Franklin Frazier's *Black Bourgeoisie* (1957) was very critical of black entrepreneurship. But entrepreneurship and community-building produced very successful future generations and opportunity structures in the past that have been buried. Contrary to popular belief, black college matriculation did not start in the late 1960s. Tiger Woods did not bring golf to black America. As noted in Marvin Dawkins's and Graham Kinloch's *African American Golfers during the Jim Crow Era*, black country clubs existed around the old South and even boasted a black PGA that could have competed with the white golf greats before Tiger Woods.

Today, commentators in the public square never would acknowledge that black enterprises in Durham, North Carolina, survived the Great Depression as other enterprises were collapsing, or that black millionaires, such as Madam Walker, lived and achieved at the turn of the century. Juliet Walker's *The History of Black Business in America* documents success from the inception of the country.

To be sure, opportunities should be open to all; thus, a continued interest in the importance of opportunity structures is necessary. But as Harold Cruse noted in *The Crisis of the Negro Intellectual,* the most successful Americans belong to groups who help them prepare for the future. This theme also runs through other groups and can be found in Joel Kotkins's *Tribes* (white Jews); Min Zhou's *Chinatown* (Chinese); and Edna Bonacich's *The Economic Basis of Ethnic Solidarity* (Japanese). But as noted by DuBois in *Economic Co-Operation among Negro Americans*, although non-black immigrants could put their enterprises in any part of the city, black enterprises were forced from the central business district to all-black areas.

Entrepreneurship among black Americans is booming in the digital age, as well as in traditional sectors. Immigrant Africans, as is true of all groups, are more likely to be entrepreneurs than black Americans. The same relationship between entrepreneurship, education of children, and success is being shaped by these new Americans. American blacks—and no one else has to do this—have to celebrate their entrepreneurial history and move away from the failure paradigm that was established in the 1970s and celebrates failure.

"Urban blacks" is only one tradition of black America. One should not seek explanation for the "plight" of black males, but instead look to the archives or Morehouse College, which has been graduating generations of blacks for over a hundred years. Martin Luther King Jr. was a third-generation Morehouse man from the prosperous Sweet Auburn Avenue section of Atlanta, and these kinds of communities existed throughout the South. His educational success originated with the entrepreneurial spirit of black America, a tradition he did not enhance during the modern civil rights movement.

Self-employment hovers around 10 percent[149] in America, and the foreign-born among all racial groups have higher rates. This pattern is being followed by immigrant Africans, and, as noted by the groundbreaking work of Princeton scholar Tod Hamilton's *Immigration and the Remaking of Black America*, immigrants are setting an old pattern of success for people of African descent. Robert L. Woodson Sr.'s *The Triumphs of Joseph: How Today's Community Healers Are Reviving Our Streets and Neighborhoods* concentrates on old values for a new black America.

I can say with a great degree of certainty that if one's great-great-grandparents were entrepreneurs, that person's family is in their fourth generation of college matriculation. The model is there to make all black Americans in the image of what self-help blacks envisioned. Of course, there are overlaps in all models, but the model of success is there and should be acknowledged and celebrated.

"LET'S ARM BLACK CHILDREN WITH LESSONS THAT CAN IMPROVE THEIR LIVES"
BY COLEMAN CRUZ HUGHES

It is often said that those who do not learn from history are doomed to repeat it. Sound advice though this may be, it does not get one very far in practice. The reason is that there is no agent called "history" which teaches unambiguous moral lessons. Study World War II and you may come away believing that nation-building works. Study Iraq and you may come away believing the opposite. In the end, the historical episodes we choose to study—and to ignore—say less about the wisdom offered by "history" and more about the lessons that we consider relevant today.

So as I read the *New York Times*' 1619 Project—a series of essays intended to reframe American history by placing "the consequences of slavery and the contributions of black Americans" at its center—I kept returning to one question: Which episodes from American history teach lessons that are most relevant to black children today? This question is not merely of intellectual interest; the CEO of the Chicago Public School system has pledged to send at least two hundred copies of the project to every high school in the city.

The essays in the project answer this question in one voice: slavery. Bryan Stevenson argues that slavery is behind the cruelty of our criminal justice system; Jeneen Interlandi says that slavery explains why

America lacks universal health care; Matthew Desmond claims that slavery explains the brutality of American capitalism; and so forth.

I support teaching Americans of all ages about the horrors of slavery. Textbooks that whitewash this history—for example, by portraying slavery as a "side issue" in the Civil War—are a moral embarrassment. But the 1619 Project is not an honest attempt to educate Americans about our history. It is an attempt to weaponize that history to fight ideological wars in the present.

There's no doubt that slavery is among the most important chapters in the American story. The 1619 Project exaggerates only slightly when it says that "no aspect of the country...has been untouched by" the peculiar institution. Yet by claiming that slavery has touched everything, the project raises a question about its own prejudice: If slavery is linked to *every* aspect of America, why single out certain institutions and not others?

The project could have argued, for example, that labor market regulation is rooted in slavery because the Black Codes[150] used occupational licensing to keep blacks in menial positions. Or it could have argued that attacks on free speech are rooted in white supremacy by citing the destruction of the black-owned anti-lynching newspaper the *Memphis Free Speech* by a white mob in 1892.[151] Yet these arguments—despite being just as plausible as those offered in the project—would have targeted two progressive-friendly values: market regulation and speech restrictionism. The absence of any such arguments in the project is, at best, suspicious, and, at worst, proof of the ideological prejudice at its core.

If the central historical claim made in the 1619 Project is that slavery has touched everything, then the lesson they want readers to learn is that—to quote the project's director Nikole Hannah-Jones—"anti-black racism runs in the very DNA of this country." As popular as this refrain has become, it's an imperfect analogy at best. For one thing, DNA, by definition, remains with you for your entire life. To say that white supremacy is in America's DNA is, therefore, to suggest that it will remain with us forever. As James Oakes, a leading Civil War historian, observed, this attitude leads to "political paralysis." By ruling out the possibility of progress, it makes nihilism the only logical option. "What do you do," Oakes asked, "alter your DNA?"

More importantly, to the typical black kid today, how relevant is the idea that racism is in our DNA? Without doubt, a variant of this idea was relevant to intellectuals such as Martin Delany and Frederick Douglass in the nineteenth century—when the debate over whether blacks should emigrate from America hinged on whether legalized white supremacy would be permanent or temporary. But that debate long since has ended, and blacks born in America are staying put. So we must ask ourselves: What good does it do to tell a black child in 2019, based on nothing but thoughtless pessimism, that the only country he'll ever live in will forever reject him?

If we are going to import heavily editorialized essays about black history into the minds of our children, then we should at least arm them with historical lessons that are relevant to the challenges they face today. One such challenge is posed by the widening gap between those with and without a college degree. Accordingly, we might highlight the heroic efforts made by formerly enslaved blacks to become educated: almost completely illiterate at the end of the Civil War, by 1910, about two-thirds of former slaves could read and write. Observing such efforts—which included forming secret schools, pooling together money to pay teachers' salaries, and, at times, voluntarily forgoing recess and holiday breaks—the national superintendent of schools for the Freedmen's Bureau remarked: "What other people on earth have ever shown, while in their ignorance, such a passion for education?"[152]

Another challenge we face today is low geographic mobility. As high-income opportunities increasingly concentrate in specific cities, Americans in general, and blacks in particular, are moving less frequently than ever before. In *The Complacent Class*, economist Tyler Cowen notes that the overall interstate migration rate is down 51 percent from its 1948–1971 average. This is partly because moving to cities has become so expensive, but as Cowen argues, it also may be because American culture has lost a certain dynamism.[153] In this vein, another episode of history we might highlight is the Great Migration, during which blacks moved en masse to the North, Midwest, and West. In 1916, over 90 percent of American blacks still lived in the South, where opportunities for upward mobility were virtually nonexistent. By 1970, only 53 percent remained there.

Instead of teaching black children lessons they can use to improve their lives—such as the importance of education and geographic mobility—the 1619 Project seems hell-bent on teaching them to see slavery everywhere: in traffic jams, in sugary foods, and, most surprisingly, in Excel spreadsheets. As Desmond puts it, "When a mid-level manager spends an afternoon filling in rows and columns on an Excel spreadsheet, they are repeating business procedures whose roots twist back to slave-labor camps."

Without doubt, America would be a very different place—in ways both large and small—if not for slavery. Yet the arguments marshalled in support of this fact too often rely on an intellectual sleight of hand that would be plain to see if applied to any other historical event. For example, the legacy of World War II includes the creation of penicillin. But few would take seriously the argument that antibiotics are "rooted in" violence.

Because arguments about history can seem pedantic, it's worth pausing to reflect on what's at stake. Most people can agree that we want to raise the next generation of Americans to be more enlightened than the last, less likely to make assumptions about others based on their race, and more focused on what unites us than what divides us. We want them to be smarter, more productive, more prosperous. In sum, we want them to be less distracted by trivial conflicts and more focused on solving problems of existential importance. Fulfilling these goals will be no simple task, and I do not pretend to have all the answers. But one thing is certain: if a century from now America has made massive strides in any of these areas, it will not be because we taught our progeny to see the remnants of slavery hiding in the rows and columns of an Excel spreadsheet.

For black Americans in particular, the stakes are equally high. In the history of multi-ethnic societies, it is difficult to find a single example in which a minority group rose from poverty to affluence by pursuing a strategy that focused primarily on nursing historical grievances (however valid), seeking atonement for them, and stigmatizing those within its ranks that advocated an inward-looking strategy. By contrast, history is replete with examples of minority groups—even ones who have suffered routine political repression and violence—rising to affluence by pursuing the opposite strategy: avoiding politics entirely and focusing single-mindedly on entrepreneurship and education.

Rarely does history offer a lesson as unambiguous as this one.

"WE LIVE IN AN
IMPURE WORLD"
BY JOSHUA MITCHELL

Among so many Americans today, there is a palpable longing for purity. Many want "clean" energy, and wish to purge the economy of "dirty" fossil fuels. In public buildings, hand-sanitizing stations stand upright everywhere. In our homes, many fear—and some with justification—that their municipal tap water is not clean enough, and so drink their water from plastic bottles. Then there are those among us who insist on eating organic foods, who shun GMO foods, or who crave "superfoods." Is concern about hygiene and purity alone the cause, or is something more ephemeral than physical cleanliness involved?

The story often told about Americans in the late twentieth and early twenty-first centuries is that they have succumbed to relativism. A more accurate account would be that quasi-religious categories of purity and stain have taken hold of the American imagination.

The material world is not the only place where this longing for purity now urgently appears. The First Amendment to the U.S. Constitution declares that "Congress shall [make no law] abridging the freedom of speech." The longing for purity in America recently has become so acute that some Americans believe citizens no longer should be subject to the unappealing ideas around them that the First Amendment protects, but rather should be protected from them, because they are "hateful." Citizens of a bustling republic cannot think this way, because they must build a world together with their fellow citizens, whether they like them or not, and whether they have impure, hateful thoughts or not. Yet many American citizens who see the world through the lens of purity and stain, and who have no real need to depend on their fellow citizens, can and do think along these lines today.

What of our nation? Is it pure or is it stained—and if it turns out to be stained, even in small measure, what then? Although generalizations never do justice to the details, those who talk about America as a "color-blind" society that endured the "accident of slavery" tend to think our nation is pure. On the other hand, others see the world through the lens of purity and stain and tend to think our nation is stained.

The 1619 Project of the *New York Times* takes this latter position. America is stained, its authors argue—and stained from its very founding. Because founding events are constitutive events, the stain cannot be removed. America's stain, therefore, is "systemic"; America is guilty of "systemic racism."

In the factional world of politics, it might be expected that those of us who offer a different vision than the one provided by the 1619 Project would propose that America is pure, rather than stained. But our project, 1776 Unites, offers no such counter-narrative. None of us asserts that America is pure. Our disagreements are not partisan counterclaims. Rather than assert that America is pure, we begin from the belief that impurity and stain are not the final word about America, as so many of our fellow citizens who are disappointed idealists of the political Left infer.

Our defense of 1776 begins from the recognition that the stain of slavery has its deeper origin in the darkened recesses of the human heart. We are neither idealists nor disappointed idealists. Rather, we have both hope and confidence that the political arrangements stipulated by the Constitution and its associated documents were and are adequate to the challenges immediately before us and our forebears, and to those that lie ahead.

More importantly, we have hope and confidence in what we dare call the redemptive story of America, which is chronicled in the lives of black Americans—but not only of black Americans—who, in word and deed, confirm that although the fires of suffering can hobble and destroy, they also can purify and make stronger. The recollection of, and reverence for, what these Americans accomplished is our most urgent task today, not only because they point the way beyond the partisan divide over the matter of stain and purity that now incapacitates us, but because they provide precious exemplars that all Americans now so urgently need in their own lives, regardless of their standing.

Let us leave aside the immensely difficult task before us, of learning—or perhaps of relearning—how to live in an impure world. Who benefits and who is harmed by the narrative of America's irredeemable stain? Why, moreover, does this narrative, so amply laid out in the 1619 Project, appear just now in our political cycle?

Since the 1960s, the Democratic Party has championed the cause of civil rights. What began as a noble, necessary intervention by the federal government into state and local affairs has mutated, as so many government programs do, into an enterprise that would be unrecognizable to its originators. Where once government intervention supplemented family, church, and other mediating institutions in black America, over the past five decades government intervention increasingly has substituted for them. This has generated a vicious cycle, in which federal government intervention is both the cause and the consequence of the breakdown of those mediating institutions—a problem Alexis de Tocqueville, author of *Democracy in America*, predicted in 1835 would plague the whole of America in the distant future.

Today, a permanent proportion of black America is the object of government intervention, the current justification for which is that it is composed of pure and innocent victims, corrupted by external forces and incapable of caring for itself without government assistance. For government intervention to continue on its now massive scale, that permanent portion must persist, held fast by the claim that "systemic racism" is so grave, so entrenched, that only government intervention can save it. The irredeemably stained world in which this portion lives is not something its members can negotiate. The government—or rather, the tens of thousands of employees arrayed across dozens of agencies, who are the unacknowledged beneficiaries—must instead "help" them.

Eric Hoffer famously wrote, "Every great cause begins as a movement, becomes a business, and eventually degenerates into a racket."[154] Government programs are necessary when the mediating institutions of society are broken. They serve the "great cause" when their aim is to help rebuild those institutions; but government programs become "a racket" when their real, if unstated, aim is to substitute for the mediating institutions that are so necessary for citizens to build lives of competence and joy.

The political implication of the claim that America has, since 1619, suffered from "systemic racism" is that the federal government must intervene in every domain of life to save innocent victims from a world that is irredeemably impure and which corrupts them. Is this the world in which we really want to live? An infantilized world, without adult perseverance and responsibility? A world without hope, a world without reverence for those whose achievements belie the suffering they have endured and overcome?

The disservice done by the need our federal government agencies have for a portion of black America to be a class of permanent innocent victims long has been observed, not least by noteworthy participants in 1776 Unites. There is an additional matter, which has not been adequately addressed, and which brings us to the current political moment: the number of groups whose members count as innocent victims has expanded exponentially since the 1960s. First women, then gays, lesbians, and bisexuals, and now the transgendered are counted among them. On what authority would these causes rest in America if the agonizing struggle to heal the wound of slavery during the civil rights era were not their backdrop?

The language we have all used to comprehend this extraordinary expansion is instructive. When black America was our concern, we spoke of government "affirmative action" programs. As more groups donned the crown of thorns that black America wore during the civil rights era, we began to hear the word "diversity." As we have pushed the conventional boundaries of sexuality to their breaking point, we now talk of "inclusion" and concern for "the marginalized." With each expansion of the number of groups of innocent victims, and with each modification of our language, we have shifted the boundary line that separates the pure from the stained. Today in America, if you wish to be "inclusive" and if you are concerned with "the marginalized," you will do well not to defend the conventional generative family containing a biological male and female, who together go to a traditional Christian church on Sunday morning. That family is "hetero-normative" and that church is "homophobic." Both are stained.

I do not wish to cast aspersions on the sufferings of others. The industrial age has brought us problems unforeseen before it arrived. We must address them thoughtfully and humanely. Can it really be the case, however, that the conventional generative black family that attends church each Sunday—the very family that was the social cornerstone on which Martin Luther King Jr. relied to awaken America from its long-cultivated slumber—no longer passes the purity test? By the logic of "inclusion," it does not. The church-going black family, once the cornerstone, has been cast off. In the New Testament, Jesus declares that the stone rejected shall become the cornerstone. More than five decades after the civil rights movements began, that cornerstone itself has been rejected by the partisans of purity.

Therein lies the reason for the 1619 Project. The partisans of purity no longer will defend the church-going conventional generative black family (or their white, Hispanic, Asian, or Indian counterparts). This category of citizens is the unfortunate but necessary collateral damage in the never-ending project of routing out, humiliating, and silencing impure Americans who are insufficiently "inclusive." To keep the vast swath of black Americans who do not pass the "inclusivity" test in the Democratic Party tent, the 1619 Project wishes to assure them that the political party that once had their back in the 1960s still does. Its underlying message is this: *Pay no attention to the fact that partisans of purity now condemn the conventional generative family and traditional Christianity, without which slavery could not have been overcome, and without which "the least among us" today have the slimmest of chances of escaping their penury. You are alone and face a vast systemic threat against which your impure and impotent families and churches are powerless. Only the agencies of the federal government can help you.*

1776 Unites rejects this view. Americans are not alone, facing a systemic problem that the federal government alone can solve. The relatively modest federal government established by our Founders supposed that citizens had competence enough to build a world together, relying on mediating institutions that sometimes can lead us horribly astray but without which we cannot live well.

We live in an impure world and must labor in hope, together.

AN EXCERPT FROM *SHAME*[155]
BY SHELBY STEELE

When I traveled to Africa back in 1970, it was partly because I had been more and more seduced by this great looming idea of America's characterological evil. It was such a summary judgment, and, at the time, still new and audacious. It had not existed in the original civil rights movement of the 1950s and early 1960s. Martin Luther King Jr. had never charged America with an inherent and intractable evil. He had lived in good faith with America, believing in reform and the innate goodwill of the American character, even as he also lived under constant threat of assassination. Still, when his assassination actually came to pass—with almost macabre predictability—young blacks, like myself (and many whites as well), saw it as a final straw. The evil character of America would always prevail over decency.

I came of age—in my early twenties—precisely when this idea began to take hold. Suddenly it was everywhere among the young. Belief in America's evil was the new faith that launched you into a sophistication that your parents could never understand. And in linking you to the disaffection of your generation, it made youth itself into a group identity that bore witness to the nation's evil and that, simultaneously, embraced a new "counterculture" innocence. Coming out of this identity, you owed nothing to your parent's conventional expectations for your life. You could go to medical or law school if you wanted, but you could also roll in the mud at Woodstock, do drugs, or join a commune.

A result of this generation's explicit knowledge of America's historical evils was to make social and political morality a more important measure of character than private morality. In the 1950s, your private morality was the measure of your character; in the 1960s, your stance against war, racism, and sexism became far more important measures—so important that you were granted a considerable license in the private realm. Sleep with whomever you wanted, explore your sexuality, expand your mind with whatever drug you liked, forgo marriage, follow your instincts and impulses as inner truths, enjoy hedonism as a kind of radical authenticity. The only important thing was that you were dissociated from American evil. Dissociation from this evil became a pillar of identity for my generation.

But I was from the working class. I had put myself through college. I couldn't afford to bank my life on the dramatic notion that America was characterologically evil unless it was actually true. Africa was a continent full of new countries that had banked their fate on precisely this view of their former oppressors. I wanted to see some of these countries then led by a generation of charismatic men who had won hard-fought revolutions against their Western oppressors—Jomo Kenyatta of Kenya, Kwame Nkrumah of Ghana, and Léopold Sédar Senghor of Senegal. They were all seen as redeemers—redeemers— the selfless founding fathers of newly independent nations. And, having thrown off the yoke of colonialism, there was the expectation that their countries would begin to flourish.

But in fact, they were not flourishing. We left Algeria in the middle of the night and landed the next morning on the other side of the Sahara Desert in Lagos, Nigeria, where we—along with all the passengers on our flight—were held at gunpoint in the airport for several hours for mysterious reasons having to do with the Biafran War. Finally, we made it to Nkrumah's Ghana, which only looked more and more bedraggled and directionless—a sharp contrast to the revolutionary glory that Kwame Nkrumah had projected around the world. (Kwame was fast becoming a popular name for male babies among black Americans.) Food was scarce and unrelievedly bad even in the American hotel in the capital city of Accra. You saw chickens pecking for food in open sewers, and then at dinner, you wondered at the gray meat on your plate smothered in nondescript brown gravy. Then there were ten days in Dakar, Senegal, where Senghor, the father of "negritude," was president. But it wasn't "negritude" that made Dakar a little more bearable than Accra. There were still some French there, and it was their fast-fading idea of Dakar as an African Paris that meant better food and the hint of café society.

The Africa we saw was, at best, adrift. The Africans themselves—as opposed to the Middle Eastern and European shopkeepers and middlemen—looked a little abandoned. Today I would say they were stuck in placelessness. They obviously didn't want to go back to their colonial past, yet, except for a small, educated elite, they had no clear idea of how to move into the future. They had wanted self-determination, but they had not been acculturated to modernity. How does one do self-determination without fully understanding the demands of the modern world?

In Dakar, an enterprising middle-aged man—someone who would surely have owned his own business had he been born in America—appeared every day outside our hotel trying to sell us the same malformed and unfinished wooden sculpture. Every day a different story and a different price attached to this "sculpture." The man was charming and quick, but I also sensed anger and impatience just beneath the surface. He scared me a little. One morning, out of sheer frustration, I gave him five dollars (a lot of money then), but then walked away without taking the sculpture. Within a minute, I felt a tug on my sleeve. Angrily, he pushed the money and the ugly little sculpture back into my hands—as if to be rid of not only me but also a part of himself he couldn't stand. Then he stormed off. I had hurt his pride, and I felt terrible. I chased him down, gave him the money again, and took the sculpture (which I have to this day). His umbrage was still visible, but he accepted the deal.

In 1970, I had no way of understanding an encounter like this. Now a few things are clear. I was conspicuously American. My voluminous Afro only drove that point home. Thus I was an emissary from modernity itself. When I gave him money without taking his sculpture, I didn't just devalue him and his culture; I virtually mocked his historical circumstance by reminding him of what he already knew: that he was outside of history, that he was not of the modern world and had nothing really to offer me that I wanted or needed. Yes, the world by then knew that African art could be world-class. Picasso, among others, had brought its genius to the West. But he would not have known about Picasso or even much about the art of woodcarving within his own culture. He wanted to be a tradesman, a businessman. But his ignorance even of what he was selling sabotaged his entrepreneurialism. So when I gave him money but rejected his statue, I treated him like a beggar to whom one gives alms, not like a businessman.

And wouldn't a man like this—and the millions like him all across Africa, the Middle East, and the Third World generally—soon be in need of a politics to fight back with? Wouldn't he need a political identity that lessened the sting of his individual humiliation by making him a member of an aggrieved collective? Wouldn't some ideology or other—nationalism, cultural nationalism, Pan-Africanism, some version of Marxism, negritude, Islamism, jihadism, any idea of "unity" that merges the individual with the group—come into play to console individual alienation by normalizing it, by making it a collective rather than individual experience? Your humiliation does not reflect on you. You languish outside of history—hawking shapeless pieces of ebony on the streets of Dakar—because you belong to a people who were pushed out of history and exploited, first by colonialism and then by neocolonialism.

Placelessness literally demands a political identity that collectivizes people, one that herds them into victim-focused identities and consoles them with a vague myth of their own human superiority. Léopold Senghor, the first president of newly independent Senegal and the father of "negritude," said, "Far from seeing in one's blackness inferiority, one accepts it; one lays claim to it with pride; one cultivates it lovingly." Marcus Garvey, a popular racialist black American leader in the 1920s, said, "Negroes, teach your children that they are the direct descendants of the greatest and proudest race who ever peopled the earth." The Islamic extremism that so threatens the world today operates by the same formula: devout followers of Allah are superior to their decadent former oppressors (mere infidels) in the West. The feminism that came out of the 1960s argued that if women were victimized by male chauvinism, they were also superior to men in vital ways. ("If women ruled the world there would be no wars" was a feminist mantra in the 1970s.)

All these identities assign a "place" against the experience of placelessness by giving the formerly oppressed an idea both of their victimization and their superiority. This "places" them back into the world and into the flow of history. You are somebody, these identities say. You were simply overwhelmed by your oppressor's determination to exploit you. Thus the consoling irony at the heart of victimization: you possess inherent human supremacy to those who humiliated you.

But there is a price for this consolation: all these victim-focused identities are premised on a belief in the chara•cterological evil of America and the entire white Western world. This broad assumption is the idea that makes them work, which makes for that sweet concoction of victimization and superiority. So the very people who were freed by America's (and the West's) acknowledgment of its past wrongs then made that acknowledgment into a poetic truth that they could build their identities in reaction to. Once America's evil became "poetic" (permanently true), the formerly oppressed could make victimization an ongoing feature of their identity—despite the fact that their actual victimization had greatly declined.

And think of all the millions of people across the world who can find not only consolation in such an identity but also self-esteem, actual entitlements, and real political power—and not just the poor and dark-skinned people of the world but also the Park Avenue feminist, the black affirmative-action baby from a well-heeled background, and white liberals generally who seek power through an identification with America's victims. Today, all these identities are leverage in a culture contrite over its past.

The point is that these identities—driven by the need for "place," esteem, and power—keep the idea of American/Western characterological evil alive as an axiomatic truth in the modern world, as much a given as the weather. In other words, this charge of evil against the white West is one of the largest and most influential ideas of our age— and this despite the dramatic retreat of America and the West from these evils. The scope and power of this idea—its enormous influence in the world—is not a measure of its truth or accuracy; it is a measure of the great neediness in the world for such an idea, for an idea that lets the formerly oppressed defend their esteem, on the one hand, and pursue power in the name of their past victimization, on the other. It is also an idea that gave a contrite white America (and the Western world) new and essentially repentant liberalism.

In this striking vision of the white Western world as characterologically evil, both the former dark-skinned victims of this evil and its former white perpetrators found a common idea out of which to negotiate a future. This vision restored esteem to the victims (simply by acknowledging that they were victims rather than inferiors) and gave them a means to power; likewise, it opened a road to redemption and power for the former white perpetrators. This notion of America's characerological evil became the basis of a new social contract in America.

Not much of this was clear to me in 1970 as we traveled through Africa. But one thing did become clearer as the trip progressed. Back home, I had been flirting with real radicalism—not radicalism to the point of violence, but radicalism nonetheless. For me that meant living a life that would presume America's evil and that would be forever disdainful toward and subversive of traditional America. It meant I would be a radical liberal living in bad faith with my country—"in it but not of it," as we used to say back then. So here in my early twenties I genuinely wondered if the subversive life wasn't the only truly honorable life. Wouldn't it be "selling out" (the cardinal sin of the counterculture) to look past America's evil and cast my fate in the mainstream?

On some level I knew, even at the time, that the trip to Africa was an attempt to resolve this dilemma. I wanted to see real radicalism in the faces of people in a society where it had actually come to hold sway. I wanted to see what it looked like as a governing reality in a real society. And this is pretty much what I accomplished on that trip. I didn't understand placelessness at the time, or the pursuit of esteem through grandiose identities. But, beginning with our encounter with the Black Panthers in Algiers, I knew that I was seeing what I needed to see. And I began to feel a growing certainty within myself. My dilemma was resolving itself. The more we traveled—a month and a half in all—the firmer my certainty became. And when we at last boarded the plane in Dakar headed for New York, I felt at peace. I was clear. The American mainstream would be my fate.

The clarity I found that trip was based on one realization: I learned that America, for all its faults and failings, was not intractably evil. In the Black Panther villa in Algiers, on those balmy afternoons eating the local shrimp, I spent time with the people who banked their entire lives on America's inherent evil—and on the inherent evil of capitalism. On one level, they were glamorous figures, revolutionaries ensconced in a lavish villa provided by the new radical government of Algeria. The impression was of a new and more perfect world order just around the corner, and these special people with the moral imagination to see it coming would soon be marching in victory.

Yet I could see that as human beings they were homesick and in despair. As revolutionaries, they were impotent and hopelessly lost. It was like seeing a pretty woman whose smile unfolds to reveal teeth black with rot. They had no future whatsoever, and so they were chilling to behold. We had all grown up in segregation. We all had war stories. And we all had legitimate beefs against America. But to embrace the idea that America and capitalism were permanent oppressors was self-destructive and indulgent. It cut us off from both the past and the future. It left us in the cul-de-sac of placelessness, though I could not have described it this way at the time. But I could see even then that someone like DC had gotten himself into the same cul-de-sac as the street hawker selling chunks of wood as art in Dakar. They were both languishing in a truly existential circumstance. And they were both consoled by a faith in the evil of America and the West.

Looking back, I now think of DC as a cautionary tale, an essentially softhearted man who had allowed himself to be captured by a bad idea—that his country was irretrievably evil. Unlike most other Black Panthers, he ended up living a long—if strained—life. Soon after I met him, the Algerian government began to tire of supporting the Black Panthers in their fast-fading glory while so many Algerians languished in poverty. At the end of July 1972, another American black, George Wright, along with four other men and women, hijacked a plane in America en route to Miami and then extorted a $1 million ransom from the Federal Bureau of Investigation. The hijackers ordered the pilots to take them to Boston and then Algeria. Eldridge Cleaver wanted the money and wrote an open letter to Houari Boumediene, the president of Algeria, in effect asking the government to continue supporting the cause of black American liberation. But the Algerian government recovered the ransom money and returned it to American authorities. Algeria's romance with the black American revolutionaries was over.

DC, who by then had made hay of his French lessons, made his way to France, where he lived for the rest of his life in exile from America and the San Francisco Bay Area that he so loved. Wanted always by the FBI, he lived an underground life even in France. He worked as a house painter in Paris and did other odd jobs. He ended up in Camps-sur-l'Agly, France, where, at the age of seventy-four, after a day spent working in his garden, he apparently died in his sleep.

I was lucky. After one of my radical kitchen-table rants against America toward the end of the 1960s, my father—the son of a man born in slavery—had said to me: "You know, you shouldn't underestimate America. This is a strong country." I protested, started on racism once again. He said, "No, it's strong enough to change. You can't imagine the amount of change I've seen in my own lifetime."

"WE MUST SCRAP THE '1619 PROJECT' FOR AN ACCURATE ACCOUNT OF AMERICAN HISTORY"
BY CHARLES LOVE

I generally assume positive intent, but that approach is being pushed to its limits by the advancement of the *New York Times'* 1619 Project in schools. I cannot understand the goal of a growing number of school districts—those charged with administering curricula to thousands of schools—agreeing to use the 1619 Project as part of their history lessons. Its founder, Nikole Hannah-Jones, has acknowledged that it is not a work of history, but rather, "of memory." She doesn't say whose memory she tapped for the project and, as is the case with most people, memories can suffer from the Mandela effect over time. Therefore, it is unwise to use memories that are hundreds of years old as the basis for a history lesson.

For example, when they want you to believe that the Revolutionary War was fought because the British intended to abolish slavery, rather than fighting to gain freedom from a monarchy that suppressed colonists' rights, they simply say this and many accept it as fact. We are expected to ignore the fact that slavery was not abolished in the United Kingdom until 1833, nearly six decades after the Declaration of Independence. This is what is dangerous about the 1619 Project:

in its effort to prove the narrative that the black existence in America is inextricably tied to slavery, the project's essayists and its proponents twist truths, omit facts, and change definitions.

Fortunately, there is a better way to approach this.

I grew up in Gary, Indiana, a city with a notoriously bad reputation—segregated in the 1950s, high in crime in the 1990s, and now poster child for economic devastation in America's Rust Belt. When I was in my early twenties, I worked for a caterer in downtown Chicago. My co-workers were also young black men. They were all from Chicago, mostly from the South Side. I vividly remember them reacting to my being from Gary by saying, "Wow, and you've never been shot?" It was the early nineties and Gary had been dubbed the "murder capital of the country." However, like the narrative we hear about most blacks today, this was not our normal existence in Gary.

When I look back on my childhood, I can't help but recall key moments that created a snapshot in time that drastically changed how I viewed the world. I started school in the mid-1970s. Most of the white families had moved away after the election of Richard Hatcher, the city's first black mayor and one of the first to win election in a major city nationwide. I was born at the beginning of the now infamous "white flight."

The remaining residents of Gary were a pretty even mix of working-class and poor families; my family was barely on the working-class side. This was not much different from majority-black communities in America today. What we benefitted from at that time was an enriched education. During my years in public schools, most of my teachers were black and, although most were women, we did have several male teachers, a surprisingly high percentage by today's standard.

Since most of the white teachers were holdovers who did not succumb to the rush to leave the city, they skewed older. Conversely, most of the black teachers were in their twenties and early thirties when I began school. This meant that many of them were in high school or college at the height of the civil rights movement. What they instilled in me and my peers is what is lacking in the 1619 Project: context and logic.

These students of the movement wanted to empower the children they taught. Like most people today, we knew about slavery, Jim Crow laws, and Martin Luther King; however, our teachers gave us a richer understanding of our history. We were taught about Hiram Revels, a minister who became the first black senator; King adviser and activist Bayard Rustin; and labor leader A. Philip Randolph. I remember having flash cards that featured inventor Garrett Morgan, explorer Matthew Henson, and surgeon Daniel Hale Williams.

We were taught about the ugliness of white supremacy, but not allowed to use it to generalize whites, so that we would not become like the racists we opposed. When taught about slaves who took immeasurable risks, such as Harriet Tubman and Frederick Douglass, we also learned about white abolitionists John Rankin and John Brown, educator Samuel Gridley Howe and his wife, writer Julia Ward Howe, and the Radical Republicans, whites who put their reputations, prominence, and, in some cases, their lives on the line to end slavery.

While this is the most appropriate and complete way to teach this subject, it is important to note that this was not a highlight of my formative education, but rather the method used for a small part of it. My teachers' primary focus was to give us the skills and knowledge necessary to compete and be successful, regardless of our race or our circumstances. This is something that all students—especially black students—would benefit from, but the 1619 Project is simply not designed to do that.

Right from the start, the *New York Times* states that the goal of the project is "to reframe the country's history by placing the consequences of slavery and the contributions of black Americans at the very center of our national narrative." Although the project rightly describes slavery, the realities are far worse—no words could properly "delineate the atrocious debasement of human nature" as Benjamin Franklin once said. The 1619 Project's lack of context leaves an exaggerated imprint of slavery on the arc of history in America.

Additionally, the illogical conclusion the essayists draw from the history of racism is equally damaging. The conclusion the project paints for its readers is that our country was founded on slavery, whites fought to keep it, and, when slavery ended, they spent 150 years trying to maintain strength through systemic oppression of blacks. In addition to this, the "consequences of slavery" determined by the 1619 Project can be summed up as every problem ever experienced by blacks in America.

It is easy to find evidence and examples to prove the harsh racism the project describes; there are too many from which to choose. The problem lies with the assumption that racism is endemic to white America. It is irrational to conclude that all, or even most, whites supported slavery. The project lists 1619 as the start of slavery—and thereby, the country—but fails to mention the efforts to end slavery that also began in the seventeenth century. Talk of ending slavery was so common by the country's founding that Thomas Jefferson and other Founders assumed it would end in their lifetimes.

Arguing that slavery is the only measure to use to gauge the country, even in the 1860s, would be akin to saying the twenty states that had no slaves were not part of America, or erasing whites who fought against slavery from the history books because they don't fit the narrative. Blacks reached a level of achievement in the early twentieth century that can be described only as amazing, based on where they were fifty years earlier. Many of them owned businesses, graduated from colleges and universities, and amassed incredible wealth. How, then, does the 1619 Project contend that slavery is still the prevailing issue in the black condition today?

The 1619 Project would be more credible if it had anything positive to say about America. Instead, it takes the "throw-it-all-out approach." The Founders, capitalism, "law and order"—all are racist, according to this thinking. Even things such as traffic jams and opposition to universal health care can be traced to slavery. The project goes on like this, focusing solely on negativity without offering any solutions. Many whites read these essays and are drawn to the logical conclusion that most blacks in America lead bleak, sad lives.

This is not only incorrect, but an unhealthy way to view blacks.

Yet that is what the 1619 Project does. With no context, it tells whites, deliberately or not, that they have wronged blacks just by being born; they must embrace their guilt and renounce their "privilege." Conversely, it tells otherwise happy blacks that they should be angry for being forced to live a sad life they did not realize they were living. Once this toxic message, which is based on critical race theory, is allowed in schools, we inevitably will have a generation of angry blacks and depressed whites. Yet the push to make this part of a new standard in the teaching of American history to vulnerable youths is gaining momentum. Critical race theory teaches that all situations and outcomes are the result of a racial power struggle between the oppressed and the oppressors. It allows for no individual agency.

This warped teaching is being done without involving parents or discussing the merits of the project. Most blacks over the age of forty can remember their parents' talk on racism. It commonly involved an acknowledgment of racism, followed by a demand that we must "work twice as hard" to achieve. Their method gives cover to those who don't achieve or those who choose not to try.

I suggest we take a different approach than the critical race theory approach of the 1619 Project; instead, let's take the one my teachers took when I was a child. We learned an accurate account of American history, without negative inferences or making slavery the primary focus of our education. If schools adopt critical race theory, they will sadly rob students of the opportunity to receive an education that prepares them for the future and makes them proud to be American.

"CRITICAL RACE THEORY'S DESTRUCTIVE IMPACT ON AMERICA"
BY CAROL M. SWAIN

Under the guise of a venture called the "1619 Project," revisionist history about race in America is being introduced into classrooms across America without undergoing the normal peer review expected of educational materials. August 2019 marked the birth of the project, a publication of the *New York Times Magazine* and the Pulitzer organization, containing a collection of essays and artistic works to commemorate the four-hundred-year anniversary of slavery in America. The project has mushroomed into a movement to re-educate Americans via newfangled claims about how deeply racism is embedded in America's core.

As of February 2020, five public school systems had adopted the 1619 Project's curriculum district-wide, and its free teaching materials had reached 3,500 classrooms.[156] This rapid progression for distribution of teaching materials created by journalists and scholars has been done without proper vetting. There has been no standard review process or serious effort made to address the many concerns raised by distinguished subject-matter critics from elite universities. The rush to get these materials into America's classrooms proceeded recklessly.

What has ensued is a new racial narrative that places black America's struggles at the feet of the nation's white Founding Fathers.

This requires a new birthdate for the nation. Instead of July 4, 1776, when the Founders signed the Declaration of Independence, pledging to risk their lives, fortunes, and sacred honor to found a new nation, the 1619 Project scholars place the inception of the nation more than 150 years earlier—at 1619. That's when the first Africans came to Virginia as indentured servants before becoming free blacks.

Curiously, and inexplicably, the revisionist narrative skips over the forty-two years of indentured servitude that enabled the former slaves to gain the freedom and resources to become the foundation of the free black population in America.

Jake Silverstein of the *Times* has written that the arrival of enslaved Africans "inaugurated a barbaric system of chattel slavery that would last for the next 250 years."[157] Conspicuously absent from the dominant historical narrative is the fact that free blacks and Indian tribes were right there alongside whites, buying and selling slaves after slavery became legal in 1661.

Historian Philip Foner, in his book *History of Black Americans*, provides critical details that American students should know about the origins of slavery in America:

The fact that the early Negroes imported into Virginia held the status of indentured servants is shown by the records of some Negroes' receiving the customary "freedom dues" in the form of land at the end of their term of service. Some obtained land after becoming free by importing servants under the "head-right" system, by which they obtained 50 acres for each servant imported. A small number of Negro landowners not only held black servants, but were sufficiently prosperous to pay the transportation costs of white indentured servants, through each of whom they could obtain 50 acres of land. Anthony Johnson, who was imported into Virginia in 1622, accumulated property after he ended his indentured period, and even though he lost all his holdings in a fire, was able by 1651 to import five black servants into the colony, for which he was granted 250 acres in Northampton

County. About 1650, Benjamin Dole, a Negro, was granted 30(
of land in Surry County for having imported six servants. An ...
Negro was granted 550 acres after importing 11 people.

Clearly, this account differs substantially from the narrative advanced by the 1619 Project contributors. What some of them hope to do is to build a case for monetary reparations for descendants of slaves. This is a false hope that would not address the problems many blacks have today, or the enormous progress black Americans overall have made.

Those who push white guilt and black victimhood ignore critical facts. One is that today's white Americans are not responsible for the sins of generations ago. Second, slavery was an institution that blacks, Native Americans, and whites participated in as slaveholders. There's plenty of guilt to go around there.

Critical Race Theory and the Diversity Inclusion Industry

Critical race theory is an analytical framework to analyze institutions and culture. Its purpose is to divide the world into white oppressors and non-white victims. Instead of traditional forms of knowledge, it uses personal narratives of marginalized minority "victim" groups (blacks, Hispanics, Asians) as irrefutable "evidence" of the dishonesty of their mostly white heterosexual oppressors. The ultimate goal of this theory's proponents is to remake society so that the victim class eventually displaces the oppressors and becomes the new ruling class.

Within this framework, white privilege and its unearned benefits are responsible for economic, health care, and social disparities in minority communities. It advances a narrative of blame that declares white America guilty for the plight of blacks. When it comes to education, members of the victim classes do all the teaching. It is a worldview and narrative that commands white people to sit in obedience and listen quietly to the arguments about their unjust gains as well as their obligation to provide a remedy for—in this case—black Americans, whether they are descended from slaves or not.

There is no way out for whites when it comes to race. Critical race theory assumes that racism is permanent and affects every aspect of our society, including political, economic, social, and religious institutions. The theory further advances the belief that being born with white skin, in itself, gives unearned privileges. Therefore, any expectation of societal attainment of color blindness, in which race or ethnicity does not hinder opportunities, is impossible to achieve. Neutrality in law and decision-making is a pipe dream that can never be attained. Thus, this mistaken reasoning goes, the oppressive system must be dismantled and destroyed.

This flawed theory suggests that race and ethnicity will always taint and pollute every decision, and, as a result, racial minorities will consistently lose out to whites because of structural racism. The message is clear: if you are unfortunate enough to be born with black skin, you are forever a second-class citizen who pays a race penalty. Under this rationale, the most affluent blacks rank below the poorest whites when it comes to privilege and opportunities. We are asked to believe that more than fifty years of affirmative action programs and race consciousness have done nothing to change the trajectory or opportunities of people born without white skin. Critical race theory says every dysfunctional condition in black, urban communities can be traced to slavery and its aftermath. There is no place for individual-choice initiative.

What critical race theory actually "accomplishes" is to create anger, frustration, and despondency among persons in the victim categories who internalize the destructive message.

Universities and colleges have created a cottage industry of people who profit from indoctrinating America's future leaders with a dangerous and destructive ideology. These future leaders then spread this diseased ideology, like a virus without an antidote, into corporate boardrooms as well as K–12 public and private schools, both Christian and non-Christian. Standards normally used to reward academic credentials are sometimes relaxed to give more authority to watered-down factors such as "personal experience" and the narrative of victim-class members and less credence to whatever facts, science, and contrary data that persons from the "oppressor" class might dare to proffer.

Education is now about white privilege indoctrination. According to the narrative, all white Americans are guilty oppressors who have benefitted from their white skin even if their parents are, say, Appalachian poor or high school dropouts working at the local big-box franchise store (if employed at all). Once the oppressor label is applied, accepted, and internalized, a deadly silencing ensues. In some cases, animated videos with messages of white guilt and oppressions shown to middle and high school students create damaging images where whites are taught guilt and minorities are assigned permanent and debilitating victimhood.

One notorious example of the "teaching" materials for diversity and sensitivity training is a short YouTube video entitled "The Unequal Opportunity Race." It has had more than 1.3 million views as of this writing. Its crippling message is clear: white boys and girls have unfair advantages, and white-imposed roadblocks prevent black boys and girls from achieving success.

Last year, the office of instruction for Westfield (NJ) Public Schools approved a course on "Power, Privilege, and Imbalance in American Society." Learning objectives of the semester-long, two-credit course include how to:

- Analyze and evaluate how white supremacy has been established in American society and the ways it continues to impact the African American, Native American, Hispanic, and Asian communities today; and

- Identify the concept of race and differentiate between the terms "racism," "prejudice," "dejure" and "de facto segregation," "institutional racism," "personal racism," "tolerance," and "intolerance."

The syllabus explains that critical race theory is a theoretical concept that emerged from the civil rights movement. The goal is to "give voice to groups who have suffered from systemic oppression, and develop theoretical and practical ways for students to deconstruct the power structures."

Messages Matter

The 1619 Project is a misguided effort to keep open historical wounds while telling only half of the story. It is flawed because it is connected to critical race theory and the diversity-inclusion grievance industry that focuses on identity politics and division. Blaming today's families for the mistakes of our ancestors is not a prescription for unifying the country or empowering racial and ethnic minorities.

We can do better. Within Christian communities, there is a basis for countering destructive narratives that have invaded our educational institutions and corporate world. The solution for hatred, bitterness, and distrust can be found in New Testament principles. Rather than wallow in the past and revisionists' efforts to build a case for reparations, we, as Americans, need to move forward while practicing the forgiveness and love of neighbor that Jesus espoused. We need not look any further than the "golden rule" (do unto others as you would have them do unto you) to find the tools that enable us to transcend racial and ethnic conflicts that keep us from working together and celebrating our victories. Our present approach cripples members of the designated victim groups while creating new victims among those classified as oppressors.

I speak from a personal perspective as someone who has watched the changes from many vantage points. I reached my formative years before critical race theory and cultural Marxism gained a dominant foothold. Even though I was born and grew up in rural southern poverty during the era of segregation, I was not taught to hate white people or to hate America. Instead, my black teachers stressed our need to work hard and excel. I grew up to be a proud American who never doubted she lived in the greatest country in the world. No one around me encouraged me to see myself as a victim. I never fixated on the fact that I was black, poor, and female. Had I done so, I doubt I would have achieved anything.

"STRAIGHT OUT OF THE BLACK BOURGEOISIE: LESSONS FOR THE TWENTY-FIRST CENTURY"
BY JOHN SIBLEY BUTLER

This is the story of the black bourgeoisie. You may not ever have heard of it, but it is a story of a successful ecosystem, created under legal segregation and at the inception of the country by free blacks. It consists of a strong dedication to business enterprise, education, and organizations that propel children to success. It is grounded in the structure of America and has survived time and great change. Although this model has not been front and center of public attention, it contains an outline of success for black America going forward.

Strategies of "Free Blacks"

I am a product of the black bourgeoisie, and have always worn its history and value on my sleeve. In her book, *The Bourgeois Virtues: Ethics for an Age of Commerce*, Deirdre McCloskey notes that market economies are good for us, and it was the values of the bourgeoisie that set the stage for economic growth in America. We can thank our forebears for adopting a framework that placed us where we are today. They did this in the face of true racial hostility, when they were not allowed to locate their enterprises in the main section of cities with other merchants. Yet the black bourgeoisie persevered, during and after slavery, because they concentrated on education, enterprises, and the maintenance of their value structure.

The black bourgeoisie had its origins in free blacks, during the slavery years, with their strategy of building strong communities and private high schools and colleges. They lived in the North and South, although the southern portion blossomed after the Civil War. When I wrote a piece for the *Austin American-Statesman*, "Celebrating the Black Bourgeoisie," my email box quickly filled with comments from people who were shocked to learn that members of my group—the black bourgeoisie—are today in their third and fourth generations of college matriculation, have never lived in "ghettos," and instead created towns of their own with thriving enterprises.

In cities, they created business enclaves that stood at the center of their mission of economic opportunity and education. W. E. B. DuBois, in his 1898 book, *Economic Co-Operation among Negroes*, called this "the group economy." These communities put business enterprise at their center, and business owners were the heroes who set their visions for the future. In his 1911 book, *The College-Bred Negro American*," DuBois's data showed that children were launched into communities by parents who were professionals and business owners—those who represented the core of the early black bourgeoisie. As noted by Margo Jefferson in *Negroland: A Memoir*, the DNA of the bourgeoisie was embedded in organizations that were founded at the turn of the century and passed along to future generations.

These organizations include Jack and Jill, for young people to attend college, the National Council of Negro Women, and the National Negro Business League. Over the years, these organizations—and others—have had a great impact on the development of black Americans. The civil rights movement of the 1960s, in its own way, was a black bourgeoisie movement; the leaders came from these communities and displayed the influence of community organizations. Dr. Martin Luther King Jr., for example, was a third-generation

Morehouse graduate and member of the Alpha Phi Alpha fraternity. He came from the economically secure Auburn Avenue community in Atlanta. Ralph Abernathy was born on a five-hundred-acre farm in Linden, Alabama, attended Alabama State University and Atlanta University, and was a member of Kappa Alpha Psi. Bayard Rustin went to Wilberforce University.

These leaders, and many others, started their educational track at colleges—and would go on to get advanced degrees at major universities—that were established by ex-slaves who put education and business at the center of their vision. The civil rights movement benefited mostly the children of the early black bourgeoisie, whose greatest contribution, perhaps, is that before desegregation they educated their children.

I Speak from Experience

I am from the southern black bourgeoisie, which took the culture to its fullest under legal segregation. This meant understanding some of the distresses of the system and its benefits. The distress was that black businesspeople were not allowed to put their enterprises in business sections of cities; the benefit was that it allowed for the coming together of like-minded people who recognized the benefit of their culture and an ecosystem based on success. It sheltered black bourgeois children from the racist value structure of southern white America.

When I was coming of age, I entered a network of strong families, private and public colleges and universities, communities with great business enclaves, churches that supported black educational institutions, and role models who had experienced abundant success.

Thus, when I applied to college—seeking to be the fourth child in my family to attend, and to be a fourth-generation college graduate—the value structure had been set by ex-slaves just a hundred years after slavery. My network in southern Louisiana consisted of a high school where all teachers had master's degrees, outstanding business people, and professors at Dillard and Xavier universities in New Orleans and Southern University in Baton Rouge. My siblings had attended Dillard, Southern, and Indiana University.

This bourgeoisie network was present in all southern states—business and education produced great communities, trade school graduates, and college graduates. As noted by Daniel Thompson, professor at Dillard, in his book *A Black Elite: A Profile of Graduates of UNCF Colleges*, "Not only have most of the black college graduates in this study moved far beyond their parents…[but] their overall success is indeed comparable to that of their white peers from much more affluent socio-economic backgrounds."

The importance of the black bourgeoisie for black Americans is rarely acknowledged and, when it is, it is often turned into a negative. First published in 1957, E. F. Frazier's *Black Bourgeoisie* criticized blacks for starting private colleges and universities, joining organizations, and thriving in a market economy. Most blacks in this tradition hide all of this and, unlike me, do not "wear it." Intergenerational college graduates and economic stability are accused of being "white" attributes, and some act as though they should not exist in America. Blacks today routinely announce that they're from "the ghetto," as if to say that makes them better than other blacks. The mainstream media hardly ever highlight black achievement, as noted in George Fraser's book, *Success Runs in Our Race*.

I felt the "success backlash," and realized how my culture of education and excellence had been put on the back burner of society's cultural awareness when I arrived for graduate school at Northwestern University. I was seen as being from "the segregated South" and somehow not understanding the "freedom" that black northerners had. I was introduced to the woman, who would become my wife, with the words: "Meet John Butler—he is just off the plantation." As a southern black bourgeoisie, I was shocked to find that most northern blacks grew up with no system of black private colleges or great communities that were built by blacks.

I was accustomed to my parents dragging me to every football game at Southern University, their alma mater, and interacting with other successful black families. We visited Jackson State in Mississippi, Tennessee State in Nashville, and Prairie View in Texas. The visit to Grambling was always tense because my grandparents finished from Grambling and hated Southern University. I remember being in awe as we visited others in Houston and Nashville.

The cloud of legal segregation always hung above us; I remember when Southern played Alabama A&M at an off-campus field and we all went to the "Southern side" of the stadium. But because ten whites chose to attend the game, we were told to get up and move across the stadium, leaving the few whites to occupy one entire side.

Strong Foundations

Despite segregation, black culture was strong. Even today, I have to defend to my southern black bourgeoisie network why I chose Louisiana State, which was not a black bourgeoisie university, over Morehouse or Xavier as my undergraduate institution.

To be sure, not all black southerners—or black northerners, for that matter—enjoyed the results of my particular socialization. But it was available to all. To join the bourgeoisie, you simply had to adopt the culture and then make contributions to it.

The bourgeoisie tradition always has been important for Americans' success, regardless of race. In *The Crisis of the Negro Intellectual*, Harold Cruse notes that when one talks about racial integration, one must understand which type of whites one will chose to associate with— because not all whites have achieved. Those who have achieved belong to strong groups that value business, education, and the building of institutions to launch the next generation. Nancy Isenberg explores this theme in her book, *White Trash: The 400-Year Untold History of Class in America*. Different white ethnic groups built a business community base to launch the next generation. As she notes, "Everybody wants a ghetto to look back on." In the case of blacks, to be sure, one has to decry the ugliness of legal racial segregation but applaud the consequential development of communities with an emphasis on business and education.

Two case studies in particular underscore the importance of black bourgeoisie culture and its effect on black Americans. In 1899, DuBois published his landmark "The Philadelphia Negro," the first study to document the impact of racism on blacks who had moved to Philadelphia. He documented crime, poverty, drug addiction, and other issues that Philadelphia's Negro population dealt with that added to the social blight of community. There was no bourgeoisie culture built into the community.

In 1911, Booker T. Washington published *Durham, North Carolina: A City of Negro Enterprises*. He noted that Durham "offers none of the color and creative class life we find among Negroes in New York City. It is a city of fine homes...and middle-class respectability. It is not the place where men write and dream, but a place where black men calculate and work.... As we read the lives of the men in Durham who have established the enterprises, we find stories paralleling the most amazing accounts of the building of American fortunes. These men have mastered the technique of modern business and acquired the spirit of modern enterprise."

These entrepreneurs helped to build and support North Carolina College, which was right in the middle of the community, and many of the black private schools in North Carolina. Hillside High School had such a great reputation for sending children to college that the community refused to close it during the desegregation court cases, arguing that their black school was the best high school in Durham. The community really celebrated when, in 1944, a secret game was created under the walls of segregation so that the North Carolina College for Negroes could play the powerful white Duke University team located on the other side of town. The result? The North Carolina College for Negroes crushed Duke in the game, and the community celebrated like they'd won a Super Bowl.

A comparison of Washington's work on Durham and DuBois's work on Philadelphia shows the importance of creating business-based bourgeois communities. For Durham, the legal word was segregation, but it blossomed because of the acceptance of bourgeoisie culture. Since I wear the success of my bourgeoisie group on sleeves, one of my goals has been to create the analog of bourgeois: self-help structures that produce excellent black communities—some of which are now troubled. I think that black Americans occupy the best land in the Western world, many of them living in cities that are troublesome now, but that could thrive in the future with an infusion of bourgeoisie culture.

Redefining "Gentrification"

Throughout the South, and in some northern cities, historians have documented how black communities turned segregation upside down, building structures and institutions to serve future generations. Remember that the term "gentrification" simply means "in the bourgeoisie tradition," or more simply, "people of means." It really has nothing to do with whites moving into black neighborhoods, as many people believe. People of means in black America helped to create great communities and, with the right vision, people today could create and revive communities.

Indeed, the process is already under way. As Woodson Center founder and President Robert L. Woodson Sr. has noted, Rev. Blake "Buster" Soaries has "recreated" Washington's Durham in New Jersey, with the Central Jersey Community Development Corporation.

This CDC serves as a national showcase. Thirty years ago, when the Woodson Center sponsored my research on the historic black district of Durham, Rev. Soaries was often part of our discussions.

Preserving the Culture

Black bourgeoisie culture can be utilized in all northern cities—and certainly needs to be revitalized in the South. Can you imagine Cleveland and Detroit, for example, having a private school like Hampton University or Miles College? Can you imagine black Americans creating a real estate trust and buying the land of central cities and turning them into the Durham that Booker T. Washington described? Can you imagine—as T. M. Pryor did in his groundbreaking book, *Wealth Building Lessons of Booker T. Washington for a New Black America*—a black America that completely embraces market economies for the twenty-first century? Can you imagine communities that again launch children who are well educated and have a black bourgeoisie flair into the larger society?

One of the great books on bourgeoisie culture, race, and segregation is Min Zhou's *Chinatown*. Professor Zhou took on scholars who referred to Chinese living in Chinatown as being "segregated" and exploited by Chinese enterprises. She notes that Chinatown represents a business enclave where the Chinese can understand the importance of business enterprise, start their own businesses, and launch future generations to outstanding educational careers.

I continue to be amazed when newspapers note that a person was "very successful…but was born in the segregated South." I continue to recoil in horror at how blacks are presented in the national media, and how the *New York Times* introduced us to The 1619 Project, which ignores the history of my tradition and presents blacks as going from slavery to poverty, with no role models.

But I realized that perhaps most Americans grew up in places that have never seen successful black educational institutions and powerful black communities. I am happy to be from the segregated South, where private colleges and great communities flourished because the ex-slaves who created them had a vision for black excellence. Most of the older bourgeois enclaves of the South have faded into memory, but the organizations, institutions, and value structure remain. Although we attend different colleges and universities, the original black colleges and universities produced 50 percent of all black judges, doctors, and attorneys, 13 percent of black CEOs, and a host of other successful people. Not bad for the southern bourgeoisie tradition.

Recently a friend called to discuss a problem. Originally from Chicago, but living in Austin, he said his daughter received a full scholarship to Baylor University. Then his wife and daughter visited Spelman in Atlanta, and his daughter refused to go to Baylor on the full scholarship. Now, with travel and other expenses, he is paying more than $50,000 a year for her to attend Spelman. I said, "Welcome to my tradition—been a black southern thing for a mighty long time."

Most know what it means to be "Straight Outta Compton." Though my culture likely will never make it to the silver screen, "Straight Out of the Black Bourgeoisie" is a great model, a tradition worth copying for the twenty-first century. It inspires people to achieve, with a motto of success.

"FIRST BLACK OLYMPIC CHAMPION, ALICE COACHMAN: THE LITTLE GIRL FROM THE RED HILLS OF GEORGIA"

BY STEPHEN L. HARRIS

In 1996, the United States Olympic Committee honored America's greatest living Olympic champions as part of the centennial of the modern Olympic Games. The USOC, in collaboration with Xerox Corporation, published my book, *100 Golden Olympians*. Among the champions, I was most honored to interview and write the story of Alice Coachman, the first black woman to capture a gold medal, who died in 2014 at age ninety.

In baseball parlance, Olympic high jumper Coachman had, in the 1948 London Games, two strikes against her in the bottom of the ninth inning with two outs, and it certainly looked like the third and final strike was on its way.

The first strike was that Coachman was an African American woman. No black woman had ever won an Olympic gold medal. In fact, in the 1948 Games, no American women had yet won a track or field event, and the United States was down to its last chance. The second strike was a formidable field that included Great Britain's Dorothy Tyler, a twenty-eight-year-old who in 1936 had been robbed of the gold medal and was anxious to win what she thought was rightfully hers, and France's powerful, multi-talented Micheline Ostermeyer, already the winner of the discus and shot put. The potential third strike was a severe injury that had forced Coachman out of the sprints and threatened to keep her from performing at her best.

With eighty-five thousand people crammed into London's Wembley Stadium, the odds of winning seemed a long shot for a country girl who had first started jumping in her bare feet.

Alice Coachman was born on November 9, 1923, in Albany, Georgia. Her father, Fred "Doc" Coachman, was a hard disciplinarian who handed out whippings when his children were disobedient. "Papa didn't want me to be an athlete," Alice said. "He thought I'd break my neck."

But she loved "running, skipping, and jumping," and the moment her household chores were done, she slipped out the back door in her bare feet, jumped a four-foot-high wire fence, and raced to the playground to compete against the boys.

"I got a lot of whippings because I ran off without asking," she said. "Papa wanted his girls sitting on the porch when the sun went down."

When she was sixteen, Coachman competed in the 1939 Tuskegee Relays, a track meet for African Americans that was similar in those days to the Penn Relays. The meet was divided into high school and college competitions. Wearing tennis shoes for the first time, Coachman won both competitions in the high jump. "I would have rather jumped without the tennis shoes," she said. "They felt funny and were too tight."

Coachman then took part in the national championships in Connecticut. It was a long trip for a country girl and she was terribly excited. But she won, and for the next ten years captured every national Amateur Athletic Union (AAU) high jump championship.

From 1942 to 1948, she won three hundred-yard-dash titles. She also was a two-time AAU indoor sprint champion. At Tuskegee Institute, she ran track, starred on the basketball team, marched in the drill corps, sang in the choir, and worked to help pay for her room and board.

"I loved the choir so much," she said, "that sometimes I would miss my dinner because practice started at six o'clock every night."

World War II cancelled the Olympic Games in 1940 and 1944. When they resumed in 1948, Coachman was twenty-five years old. During the Olympic Trials, she withdrew from the sprints because she suffered from a painful twisted ovary. Unable to practice as hard as she wanted, she still qualified for the U.S. team. On the voyage to England, she cried. "I didn't want to go to the Olympics. I really wanted to stay home."

For the U.S. women, the track events proved disastrous. Only Audrey Patterson collected a medal, placing third in the two hundred meters.

On the day before the high jump, Coachman did not practice. Her coach was upset. She fretted that Coachman would end up losing like all the other American women. As Coachman headed onto the field, with eighty-five thousand people cheering in the stands, her coach hurried out of the stadium, unable to watch what she felt was a disaster in the making.

But Coachman "wasn't afraid or nervous. I just said, 'Lordy, if it's your will, let it be done.'"

As always, she enjoyed herself—not even knowing that she had won. In fact, she and Tyler had tied at 5–6, but because Coachman had fewer misses she was declared the winner. It was the only gold medal for the U.S. women in 1948—and the first ever by a black woman in Olympic history.

Back home, Coachman was honored with a 175-mile motorcade where blacks and whites alike cheered. In 1952, Coca-Cola then honored her by making her the first black female athlete to endorse an international consumer product.

In London, after she had won the high jump, King George VI gave her the gold medal she had earned. Thrilled, Coachman recalled, "I had won ten American championships before the Olympics, and here was the King of England presenting the Olympic gold medal to me, a little girl from the red hills of Georgia."

"KEEPING THE PROMISE OF 1776"
BY BOB WOODSON
AND IAN ROWE

"If you hold your hand closed, nothing good can come in. The open hand is blessed, for it gives in abundance, even as it receives."

—Biddy Mason, ex-slave, Los Angeles
real estate mogul, and philanthropist, c. 1870

2020 was a year to remember. On that, at least, we can all agree. For good or for ill, our nation is in the midst of a major transformation unlike anything we've seen since the 1960s. To call it a cultural crisis is not so much a moral judgment as a sociological fact; and while the United States of America perhaps seems on the verge of self-immolation, we also face an enormous opportunity to emerge from this trial by fire stronger than ever.

The essays in this book were the initial offering of the Woodson Center's 1776 Unites, a black-led movement of scholars, grassroots activists, and other concerned citizens who believe America's best days lie ahead of us. We first came together in February of 2020 to voice our commitment to the promise of the American Founding, which rests not on nostalgia or mere patriotic sentiment, but on the knowledge that its timeless principles are vital to the future happiness and prosperity of our republic.

As our essays make clear, the Founding and everything that came after it were not perfect. There have always been and are still those who have been forgotten, ignored, or even gravely harmed in and by our country, while others have enjoyed great success. Yet we are convinced that Americans fitting this description, far from being helpless victims in need of rescue, possess within themselves the very power necessary to renew their own lives and the life of our entire nation.

Today, too many people, who claim to speak for the marginalized in our society, are singularly focused on the grievance of being left behind rather than this process of renewal. The false authority of such voices is being used to undermine the values that are our country's greatest strength. In 2020, the doyenne of the grievance narrative even won a Pulitzer.

We made it clear from the start that our 1776 Unites initiative would not engage in gladiatorial debate with the purveyors of grievance such as the 1619 Project. Instead, as black Americans in whose name the very founding of our nation was being attacked, we sought to provide an inspirational and aspirational alternative that would demonstrate the values of that founding, both in our national past and today.

While the 1619 Project has plenty of vocal critics, 1776 Unites was the only black-led, non-partisan rebuke to its distortions of evidence and fatalistic attitudes towards black progress in America. We showed the damage these grievance narratives inflict specifically on black American history and identity because they obscure the victories of generations of black men and women whose contributions to American life benefitted all its people.

Forceful alternative perspectives from scholars and journalists like Glenn Loury, Carol M. Swain, Wilfred Reilly, Coleman Hughes, Jason D. Hill, Clarence Page, and John Wood Jr. identified the flaws not only in the 1619 Project's historical narrative, but also in its more insidious subtext. Their work, along with our continuing efforts to develop and promote alternative instructional materials, has emboldened parents and educators to push back against attempts to adopt the 1619 Project and similar grievance-based curricula in their school systems.

And that pushback has been felt. Beginning in September 2020, the *New York Times* quietly revised key passages of the 1619 Project essays on its website, memory-holing language about "understanding 1619 as our true founding" in favor of the more anodyne rhetoric about placing slavery at the center of our national story. This is just one particularly noticeable step backwards in a broader cultural retreat, but it represents a victory against the damaging worldview the 1619 Project espouses.

But our vision reaches far beyond those important but ultimately transitory arguments. The essays you've just read, enlightening as we hope you found them, are not the reason 1776 Unites exists. As Bob likes to say, we're a "do tank," not a think tank, and our intellectual efforts mean nothing if they don't shape and inspire grassroots action and transformation. And perhaps most importantly, that relationship is mutual: the work of our scholars and writers is deeply informed by the practical knowledge accumulated by Woodson Center partners across the country, working within their own neighborhoods to build peaceful, prosperous communities from the inside out.

Roots of Renewal

"There is another class of coloured people who make a business of keeping the troubles, the wrongs and the hardships of the Negro race before the public. Having learned that they are able to make a living out of their troubles, they have grown into the settled habit of advertising their wrongs—partly because they want sympathy and partly because it pays. Some of these people do not want the Negro to lose his grievances, because they do not want to lose their jobs."

—*Booker T. Washington,* My Larger Education, *1911*

While those Booker T. Washington called "problem profiteers" have always been with us, the modern race-grievance industry was produced by the failures of the civil rights movement as it became increasingly institutionalized. Beginning in the late sixties, funding flowed down from foundations and government agencies into the pockets of unaccountable organizations claiming to represent the poor. But despite being surrounded by armies of credentialed experts supposedly working in their interest, few low-income people ever benefited from the work of their supposed advocates.

Ironically, the problem really isn't money. Corporations and nonprofits are more than willing to throw billions of dollars at efforts claiming to combat poverty and promote racial equality. Donors to the Black Lives Matter organization (officially BLM Global Network Foundation, a project of the Tides Center) include Amazon, Microsoft, Gatorade, and the Ford Foundation. The problem, rather, is that all that money goes to the wrong places. Those millions of white guilt dollars end up just as wasted as they were fifty years ago, providing little more than cozy jobs for another generation of race experts.

Instead, we need to fund the right solutions.

While politicians and "social justice" bureaucrats may decide they can afford to double down on failed social policies, they can't stop ordinary black Americans from realizing that the programs formed in their name deliver nothing but photo opportunities and empty symbolism, with few economic opportunities other than the prospect of getting in on the race-grievance grift themselves. As crime rates soar and opportunities dwindle, it's only a matter of time before the sleeping giant of low-income black America will awake and demand genuine access to resources, opportunities, and partnerships that its self-appointed champions can't or won't provide.

One such partnership is Woodson Center's twenty-plus-year alliance with Chief Rodney Monroe, who has led the Washington, Richmond, and Charlotte city police in his decades-long career. In a treacherous political moment when radical progressive activists are trying to mainstream the idea of defunding the police, Chief Monroe's experience and vision are more needed than ever. The models of positive policing and genuine law enforcement reform he has implemented in every force under his command should serve as examples for the nation. The need couldn't be more urgent—only recently, the *Washington Post* published a heartbreaking account of the enormous crime spike in North Minneapolis, the epicenter of the protests that erupted after the death of George Floyd. As anti-police sentiment has risen, the Minneapolis Police Department has hemorrhaged officers, leaving a demoralized skeleton crew to tackle a nearly 50 percent rise in homicides.

One outraged community member, who acknowledges the reality of unpleasant, sometimes unjust behavior from local law enforcement, nonetheless laments: "We're under siege. You wake up and go to bed in fear because you don't know what's going to happen next…. And our city has failed to protect us…. Why can't I have police reform? Why can't I have law and order? Why do I have to pick and choose? I should be able to have both." Her anguish is felt by people in low-income neighborhoods across America, and her question deserves an answer.

The light in such a dark moment is that the answer is "yes." Yes, we can reform the police and improve relationships between officers and the communities they serve. Yes, we cannot only lower violent crime rates and negotiate peace in areas riven by gang violence, but we can actually increase the number of solved cases, bringing justice and some measure of solace to grieving families. We know how. But to begin, we must first bring people and institutions in these suffering neighborhoods together and equip them with necessary resources. 1776 Unites and the Woodson Center seek to do exactly that.

Black Minds Matter

> "There is fire in the flint and steel, but it is friction that causes it to flash, flame and burn, and give light where all else may be darkness. There is music in the violin, but the touch of the master is needed to fill the air and the soul with the concord of sweet sounds. There is power in the human mind, but education is needed for its development.... To deny education to any people is one of the greatest crimes against human nature. It is to deny them the means of freedom and the rightful pursuit of happiness, and to defeat the very end of their being."
>
> —*Frederick Douglass, "The Blessing of Liberty and Education," September 1894*

A peaceful and prosperous America must be built on a shared understanding of our past and the possibilities for our future that is accurate and truthful, but also celebratory and aspirational.

Nobody can deny that the horrors of slavery, the slave trade, and the violence used to enforce the color line before and after emancipation were ignored or understated for too long. None of the writers in this collection want to gloss over the genuine suffering of generations of Africans and their descendants in America in favor of romanticized morality tales. But what kind of tribute is it to those who came before

us to do the opposite, and gloss over the rich history of black achievement in exchange for a permanent sense of grievance? This is what we
mean when we talk about the "race-grievance industry": those who
profit from highlighting black suffering at every turn necessarily also
profit by suppressing the truths of black success.

Two examples we focused on early in the development of our
1776 Unites curriculum are Biddy Mason and Elijah McCoy, both
of whom found prosperity in the aftermath of emancipation. Mason
was born into slavery and lived it until her thirties, yet secured freedom for herself and her family in California, becoming a major Los
Angeles real estate holder and investor, philanthropist, and beloved
figure known to Angelenos of all races as "Grandma Mason." McCoy
was Canadian, born to black Americans who had escaped slavery and
become landowners in Ontario. Despite facing the additional hurdle
of racism in the already ultra-competitive world of postwar American
industry, McCoy secured nearly sixty patents throughout his career
with the Michigan Central Railroad and beyond. As U.S. Patent
Office researcher Henry E. Baker wrote, McCoy's "lubricating cup
was in use for years on stationary and locomotive machinery.... [I]
t would be rather interesting to know how many of the thousands of
machinists who used them daily had any idea then that they were the
invention of a colored man."

Unfortunately, remarkable figures like McCoy are still widely
forgotten, occasionally emerging for a brief mention during a Black
History Month showcase but never seriously held up as models. Even
those who know their names and the outline of their lives don't examine *why* they succeeded, the values that drove them, and the community institutions that supported them. These stories reflect the strength
of the social fabric in black America as it existed in the generations
after emancipation. What 1776 Unites seeks to accomplish with its
ongoing project of developing K–12 history and civics curriculum is
look back and examine their fortitude, document it, and demonstrate

the excellence that emerges through resilience, the American experience, and the embrace of bourgeois values.

People like Biddy Mason and Elijah McCoy overcame oppression to live rich lives and accomplish extraordinary things—and they are not isolated stories. Their powerful example needs to be recovered and reaffirmed for the rising generation of black Americans. They provide evidence for the effectiveness of traditional bourgeois values like patience, prudence, and perseverance. And we must renew these values based on how the back experience embodies them in our daily lives. It's the assault on these values, not systemic racism or the specter of white supremacy, that truly undermines our prospects for success. As we build families, communities, and institutions, we must look back on the inspirational examples from our past to find the way forward.

Another victory from a more famous ex-slave, Booker T. Washington, provided additional inspiration as we confronted racial inequality in education—a gap that exists, frankly, within a wider context of mediocre middle and high school academic achievement across all racial and ethnic groups. Washington's collaboration with the philanthropist Julius Rosenwald, who built nearly five thousand schoolhouses across the South from 1917 to 1932, is a sterling example of what a partnership between an activist with on-the-ground knowledge (Washington) and a powerful figure with the right resources and infrastructure can achieve. Researchers at the Chicago Federal Reserve argue that in the regions where Rosenwald schools were active, the achievement gap between southern-born black and white men closed by 40 percent when measured by attendance, literacy, and cognitive test scores.

Around the same time that Washington and Rosenwald were conceiving of their school project, another black education reformer, Dr. Laurence C. Jones, was collecting money in Mississippi to start a Christian school for the children of emancipated slaves and their descendants. He faced danger many times and was almost killed by suspicious white citizens during his efforts. The school Dr. Jones created, the Piney Woods School, has now been in operation for over a century—the oldest historically black boarding school in the nation. In the fall of 2020, the Woodson Center had the privilege of hosting a fundraiser for this school to ensure that it would continue its mission and have the necessary capital to operate at capacity and provide more scholarships for deserving students.

The response was incredible, and we raised well over a half million dollars, another example of the kinds of partnerships we seek to nourish. The Piney Woods School is both an embodiment of this tradition of excellence and a means of handing it down to the rising generation.

American Values in Action

"A general dissolution of principles and manners will more surely overthrow the liberties of America than the whole force of the common enemy. While the people are virtuous they cannot be subdued; but when once they lose their virtue then will be ready to surrender their liberties to the first external or internal invader.... If virtue and knowledge are diffused among the people, they will never be enslaved. This is their great security."

—*Samuel Adams, letter to James Warren, February 1779*

Where the race grievance-mongers and their context-free, ahistorical fixation on America's sins seem to seek demoralization, 1776 Unites advocates *remoralization* by elevating the achievements of the black Americans who came before us.

The constellation of taboos around race and other questions of identity that American began to call "political correctness" in the 1990s and has evolved into "wokeness" since 2012 is now, in many elite circles, a kind of substitute morality. It's no wonder then that serious conversation about virtues, moral character, and civic responsibility have all but evaporated, leaving superficial adherence to the approved platitudes about identity as the true measure of decency.

As Joshua Mitchell was writing *American Awakening*, the protests that erupted after the death of George Floyd had the character of a godless religious revival, with racism as its counterfeit form or original sin and endless, never quite efficacious, rituals of atonement performed mostly by guilty whites simultaneously desperate to confess the shame of their own racism and terrified of standing accused of racism. Fashionable language games around how to speak about race—and who should speak up at all—made this, of course, all but impossible. Even the most lavishly funded, eagerly promoted "antiracist" organization in America, Black Lives Matter, is founded on such a linguistic trap: criticize BLM and its tactics or worldview, and to many casual listeners it sounds as if you've signaled your contempt for black humanity.

But despite the cheap rhetorical tricks, it is absolutely possible—and perhaps necessary in some cases—to oppose Black Lives Matter while affirming the profound value of each black life and mind in America, and the potential each contains that transcends race and ideology. As many have said before, the opposite of racism is not "antiracism," but pluralism. This is why 1776 Unites is a nonpartisan, radically pragmatic movement: our fight is not really political, but moral and philosophical, transcending the immediate concerns of any one demographic or generation of Americans. Our national character is our national destiny.

"The arc of history is long," Dr. Martin Luther King Jr. famously said, "but it bends towards justice." Our vision of the future follows that arc, knowing the path is long but confident that America has all the tools necessary to pursue and secure genuine justice for all. The success of this pursuit cannot be measured in ink spilled or controversies provoked; the pursuit of ideals must produce more than ideas. We must measure success in the transformation of schools, neighborhoods, and individual lives. Our legacy must be more than paper.

Where Do We Go from Here?

In chapter thirteen of De Tocqueville's *Democracy in America*, he wrote, "The greatness of America lies not in being more enlightened than any other nation, but rather in her ability to repair her faults." We find this sentiment compelling because it reflects the notion that America, whatever its flaws, is unique in the world in its continual pursuit of becoming "a more perfect union."

That's why since its inception, 1776 Unites has sought to ensure that young Americans of all races understand that while racial oppression is a stain on America's story, it is actually the power of our founding ideals and our founding documents signed in 1776 that have provided our nation with the tools for self-renewal and self-betterment.

While 1776 Unites was initially formed as a black-led response to the 1619 Project, the two enterprises have taken divergent paths. As some of the most well-respected historians have said, "The 1619 Project is a travesty of history & journalism that has humiliated the *New York Times* & undermined its status as 'the newspaper of record.' No amount of self-serving flattery by dishonest editors can disguise the fact that the Project has been discredited."

By contrast, the efforts of 1776 Unites have expanded to ensure millions of young people learn about the incredible stories of innovative and inventive African Americans past and present, who faced adversity, did not view themselves as victims, and chose pathways to be agents of their own uplift.

So perhaps now the most important year we should ponder is not within a founding argument over 1619 versus 1776, but rather a year that lies ahead. Imagine it is 2076—more than a century after landmark civil rights laws were passed that outlawed discrimination based on race, and more than fifty years after the founding of 1776 Unites. What will our legacy be on the three-hundredth anniversary of the Declaration of Independence? 1776 Unites scholar Shelby Steele has observed that sometimes people who don't know how to handle their freedom will reinvent their oppression. Will that be America's story fifty years from now: a nation gripped by grievance?

Or will we be in the midst of a new awakening in which people of all races are learning to embrace the ideals of family, faith, education, entrepreneurship, and hard work, as the pathway to move from persecution to prosperity?

Now is a time for choosing.

In his prophetic 1859 "Self-Made Men" speech, Frederick Douglass laid out the path forward based on what he learned from largely unknown, heroic African American figures who triumphed over the most despicable conditions:

> The lesson taught at this point by human experience is simply this, that the man who will get up will be helped up; and the man who will not get up will be allowed to stay down. This rule may appear somewhat harsh, but in its general application and operation, it is wise, just and beneficent. I know of no other rule which can be substituted for it without bringing social chaos. Personal independence is a virtue and it is the soul out of which comes the sturdiest manhood. But there can be no independence without a large share of self-dependence, and this virtue cannot be bestowed. It must be developed from within.

Through its essays, presentations, advocacy, and curriculum, 1776 Unites has amplified the stories of black people who had and have a "self-made" mindset. They did not lift themselves by their own bootstraps. Rather, they recognized the power of mediating institutions—like family, religious institutions, schools, and community-based organizations—to shape the character of the rising generation, so that they could strengthen the muscles of resiliency and self-determination from within.

Our aim is to ensure young people of all races become architects of their own future by embracing the founding principles of this exceptional nation.

Thank you for joining us on this journey.

BIOGRAPHIES OF
CONTRIBUTING AUTHORS

Editor

Robert L. Woodson Sr.

 Robert L. Woodson Sr. is founder and president of the Woodson Center and an influential leader on issues of poverty alleviation and empowering disadvantaged communities to become agents of their own uplift. He is a frequent advisor to local, state, and federal government officials as well as business and philanthropic organizations.

His social activism dates back to the 1960s, when, as a young civil rights activist, he developed and coordinated national and local community revitalization programs. During the 1970s, he directed the National Urban League's Administration of Justice Division. Later he served as a resident fellow at the American Enterprise Institute.

Woodson is frequently featured as a social commentator in print and on-air media, including C-SPAN, CNN, *Tucker Carlson Tonight*, *Meet the Press*, *The O'Reilly Factor*, and other national and local broadcasts. He is a contributing editor to the *Hill* and the *Wall Street Journal* and has been published in influential newspapers and journals, such as *Forbes*, *National Review*, the *Washington Post*, *Milwaukee Journal*

Sentinel, Harvard Journal of Law & Public Policy, Vanderbilt Law Review, and other national and local media outlets.

He is the recipient of the prestigious John D. and Catherine T. MacArthur "Genius" Fellowship Award, the Bradley Prizes presented by the Lynde and Harry Bradley Foundation, the Presidential Citizens Medal, the 2018 William Wilberforce Award, and many other awards and honors.

Woodson is the author of several books, including *On the Road to Economic Freedom: An Agenda for Black Progress* and *The Triumphs of Joseph: How Today's Community Healers are Reviving Our Streets and Neighborhoods.*

Foreword Author

Lucas E. Morel

Professor Morel has been the John K. Boardman Jr. professor of politics at Washington and Lee University since July 1999. He taught at John Brown University from 1994 to 1999. He also teaches in the master's program in American history and government at Ashland University in Ohio, at the summer programs for the Claremont Institute for the Study of Statesmanship and Political Philosophy, and at high school teacher workshops sponsored by the John M. Ashbrook Center, the Gilder Lehrman Institute, and the Liberty Fund.

From 2008 to 2009, he was the Garwood Visiting Research fellow at the James Madison Program in American Ideals and Institutions at Princeton University.

Prof. Morel is a trustee of the Supreme Court Historical Society, former president of the Abraham Lincoln Institute, and a consultant on the Library of Congress exhibits on Lincoln and the Civil War. He was a member of the scholarly board of advisors for the Abraham Lincoln Bicentennial Commission and currently serves on the U.S.

Semiquincentennial Commission, which will plan activities to commemorate the 250th anniversary of the Founding of the United States of America.

He has written for the Los Angeles Times, Christian Science Monitor, and *Richmond Times-Dispatch*, and recently completed a book titled *Lincoln and the American Founding* for the Concise Lincoln Library series of Southern Illinois University Press, which was published on July 4, 2020.

Contributing Authors

Harold A. Black, PhD

Harold A. Black is a professor emeritus at the University of Tennessee, Knoxville. Black, a native of Atlanta, Georgia, received his undergraduate degree from the University of Georgia, and his master's and PhD degrees from the Ohio State University. He lectures, consults, and publishes extensively in the areas of financial institutions and the monetary system. His articles have appeared in publications such as the *American Economic Review*; *Journal of Money, Credit and Banking*; *Journal of Finance*; *Journal of Banking and Finance*; *Southern Economic Journal*; *Journal of Financial Research*; and the *Journal of Monetary Economics*. His consulting clients include SunTrust Bank, Chrysler Financial Corporation, National Bank of Commerce, National Credit Union Administration, Branch Banking and Trust Company, and the Mortgage Bankers of America.

Prior to joining the faculty at the University of Tennessee, he served on the faculties of American University, Howard University, the University of North Carolina at Chapel Hill, and the University of Florida. His government service includes being the deputy director of the Department of Economic Research and Analysis, Office of the Comptroller of the Currency, and a board member of the National

Credit Union Administration. He has served as a director and chairman of the Nashville branch of the Federal Reserve Bank of Atlanta.

Among his honors, he is the recipient of the Department of Treasury's Special Achievement Award, the National Urban League's Outstanding Service Award, the Distinguished Alumnus Award from the University of Georgia's College of Business Administration, the National Credit Union Administration's Exceptional Service Award, and the Chancellor's Award for Research Excellence at the University of Tennessee.

Black was awarded the 2001 John B. Ross Teaching Award for excellence in teaching and is listed in Who's Who among Black Americans and Who's Who Worldwide. Black writes an occasional article for the *Knoxville News Sentinel* and blogs at HaroldBlack. blogspot.com.

Rev. Corey Brooks

Pastor Corey Brooks is the founder and senior pastor of New Beginnings Church of Chicago and founder and CEO of Project H.O.O.D Communities Development Corporation. Pastor Brooks attended Ball State University, the University of Florida, Dallas Theological Seminary, and Grace Theological Seminary. He has been pastoring since 1990. He established New Beginnings Church of Chicago in November 2000 in the heart of Chicago's most dangerous neighborhood—his first glimpse into the despair in the city of Chicago and the catalyst to his ongoing efforts to date.

Pastor Brook's efforts received national acclaim when he spent ninety-four days living on the roof of a rundown motel located across the street from the church. It had become a center of drugs, prostitution, and violence. Within three months, he raised enough money to buy the building and tear it down. The land is now earmarked to be the location of a twenty-three-million-dollar state-of-the-art community center. The goal of the proposed community center is to offset violence, provide the support necessary to make the neighborhood a safer place, and give children the tools to reach for a brighter future.

Pastor Brooks and his wife Delilah have fully invested in the community of Woodlawn on Chicago's South Side. He and his wife are spearheading a community initiative called Project H.O.O.D. to revitalize the neighborhood. Through it, they are raising up a new generation of peacemakers, problem solvers, and entrepreneurs. Current Project H.O.O.D. programming includes a Core and Carpentry Level I course, which places participants in entry-level construction jobs post-program; an entrepreneurship course and separate business workshops for aspiring and new business owners; a coworking office space for business owners; job placement programs; and community-wide events, including the World's Largest Baby Shower.

Most recently, Pastor Brooks was appointed Illinois director for St. Francis Community Services, Inc., an organization dedicated to the needs of children and youth since 1945.

John Sibley Butler

John Sibley Butler holds the J. Marion West Chair for Constructive Capitalism in the Graduate School of Business (Department of Management). He is a professor in the Management Department and holds a joint appointment in organizational behavior in the College of Liberal Arts, where he holds the Darrell K. Royal Regents Professorship in Ethics and American Society (Sociology). His research is in the areas of organizational behavior and entrepreneurship/new ventures. His research appears in professional journals and books.

He is the Sam Barshop fellow at the IC2 Institute, an organization dedicated to the creation of new ventures throughout the world. For the last seven years, Professor Butler has occupied the Distinguished Visiting Professor position at Aoyama Gakuin University in Tokyo, Japan, where he lectures on new venture start-ups and general entrepreneurship. This past year, he was awarded the Distinguished Libra Professorship at the University of Southern Maine.

Professor Butler has served as a consultant for many firms and the U.S. military. At this time, he is a management consultant for State Farm Insurance Companies, whose corporate headquarters are in Bloomington, Illinois. In this connection, he has given lectures on general management issues of corporate America. He is also one of the distinguished professors who composed the economic advisory team of Governor George Bush's 2000 presidential campaign.

Professor Butler's research has appeared in the *Wall Street Journal*, the *New York Times*, the *Chicago Tribune*, *Time Magazine*, *U.S. News and World Report*, and other newspapers and magazines across America.

His books include *Entrepreneurship and Self-Help among Black America: A Reconsideration of Race and Economics*; *All That We Can Be: Black Leadership and Racial Integration the Army Way* (with Charles C. Moskos, winner of the *Washington Monthly* Best Book Award); *Immigrant and Minority Entrepreneurship: The Continuous Rebirth of American Communities* (with George Kozmetsky); and *Forgotten Citations: Studies in Community, Entrepreneurship, and Self-Help among Black-Americans* (with Patricia Gene Greene and Margaret Johnson). Professor Butler received his undergraduate education from Louisiana State University in Baton Rouge and his PhD from Northwestern University in Evanston, Illinois.

Robert Cherry

Mr. Cherry is a professor of economics at Brooklyn College and the City University of New York Graduate Center. His main areas of interest include race and gender earnings disparities in America, issues of poverty, low-income housing, tax reform to benefit working families, domestic relations, and immigration. These and other similar subjects are featured in his latest social policy book, published by

NYU Press under the title *Moving Working Families Forward: Third Way Policies That Can Work*.

Robert Cherry has written extensively on the subject of discrimination and race, as well as the Holocaust in Poland.

Stephanie Deutsch

Stephanie Deutsch is the author of *You Need a Schoolhouse: Booker T. Washington, Julius Rosenwald, and the Building of Schools for the Segregated South*, published by Northwestern University Press. Since the book came out in 2011, she has been a frequent speaker at Rosenwald school alumni events, at public and private schools, and at Q and A sessions after the documentary film *Rosenwald*.

She writes often for neighborhood newspapers, and her work has appeared in the *New York Times*, the *Washington Post*, and the *Millions*. She is currently writing a book about the men and women whose work was supported by Julius Rosenwald fellowships.

Stephanie lives in Washington, DC, where, for twenty years, she has served as chairman of the grants committee of the Capitol Hill Community Foundation, which raises and gives away $300,000 a year in small grants. She is married to retired television director David Deutsch. She is the mother of four grown children and grandmother to five little boys.

Yaya J. Fanusie

Yaya J. Fanusie is a consultant and researcher on national security policy and financial technology. Before working for several years as an analyst at the CIA, he taught mathematics at a high school in Washington, DC, and also worked briefly in DC's juvenile detention system. He produces a podcast that features African American Muslim storytelling called *Rhythm of Wisdom*.

Stephen L. Harris

Stephen L. Harris is the author of an award-winning trilogy about New York City's National Guard regiments in World War I. The article that is featured here is adapted from *Harlem's Hell Fighters: The African-American 369th Infantry in World War I*. He is also the author of *Rock of the Marne: The American Soldiers Who Turned the Tide against the Kaiser in World War I*.

Jason D. Hill

Jason D. Hill is a professor of philosophy at DePaul University and the author of four books, including *We Have Overcome: An Immigrant's Letter to the American People; Becoming a Cosmopolitan: What It Means to Be a Human Being in the New Millennium;* and *Civil Disobedience and the Politics of Identity: When We Should Not Get Along*. He is a specialist in ethics and American politics and has been published in major magazines, including the *Federalist*, the *American Thinker*, *Commentary Magazine*, *Spiked Magazine*, the *Hill*, and *Salon*.

He is a Shillman Journalism fellow at the David Horowitz Freedom Center, where he writes a weekly column on a wide range of topics that include American foreign and domestic policy, issues of culture and race, higher education, and the Middle East. His scholarly articles have been published in anthologies and journals in Germany, the Czech Republic, and the Netherlands.

He is writing a new book revealing our universities as sites of terror and national security threats.

Coleman Cruz Hughes

Coleman Hughes is an undergraduate student at Columbia University majoring in philosophy. Born and raised in New Jersey, he briefly attended the Juilliard School before dropping out with the intention of pursuing a career as an independent jazz/hip-hop artist. Shortly thereafter, he discovered a passion for philosophy and enrolled at Columbia.

His interests include race, politics, ethics, economics, and philosophy. His writings have been featured in the *New York Times, Wall Street Journal, National Review, City Journal,* and the *Spectator.* He has also appeared on several podcasts, including *The Rubin Report, Waking Up with Sam Harris,* and *The Glenn Show,* and has testified before U.S. Congress.

Charles Love

Charles Love is the assistant executive director of Seeking Educational Excellence (SEE), a nonprofit whose mission is to empower disadvantaged students to reach their full potential. SEE understands that education and marketable life skills are the keys to success, regardless of race.

SEE's mission is to focus on STEM and end the social justice agenda in academia. He is a radio host at AM 560, the *Answer,* the Salem radio station in Chicago. He is currently the host of the *Liberty Hour* and has hosted local shows like *Black and Right* and the *Steve Cortes Show,* as well as nationally syndicated shows like the *Joe Walsh Show* and the *Kevin Jackson Show.*

Charles is a contributing writer at *City Journal* and the author of two books, *Logic: The Truth about Blacks and the Republican Party* and *We Want Equality: How the Fight for Equality Gave Way to Preference.* His work has been featured in the *New York Post,* Real Clear Politics, and on *The Rush Limbaugh Show.* He has appeared on Fox News, Newsmax, and several local TV shows, and has spoken at several colleges. He writes frequently on race, politics, current events, and cultural issues.

John McWhorter

John H. McWhorter is an associate professor of English and comparative literature at Columbia University. He earned his BA from Rutgers, his MA from New York University, and his PhD in linguistics from Stanford. Professor McWhorter teaches courses on language change, language in society, and the history of the English language, as well as on music history.

Professor McWhorter is an author of twenty books, including *The Power of Babel: A Natural History of Language, Losing the Race: Self Sabotage in Black America, Our Magnificent Bastard Tongue: The Untold History of English*, and *Words on the Move: Why English Won't—and Can't—Sit Still (Like, Literally)*. He writes for the *Atlantic* and hosts *Slate*'s language podcast *Lexicon Valley*.

Joshua Mitchell

Joshua Mitchell is currently professor of political theory at Georgetown University. From 2002 to 2005, he was the chairman of the Government Department. In 2005, he was on the start-team for Georgetown's School of Foreign Service in Doha, Qatar, and has taught courses there periodically for the past fourteen years. During the 2008–2010 academic years, Dr. Mitchell took leave from Georgetown and became the acting chancellor of the American University of Iraq, Sulaimani (see https://www.auis.edu.krd/).

His research interest lies in the relationship between political thought and theology in the West. In 1993, his book, *Not by Reason Alone: Religion, History, and Identity in Early Modern Political Thought*, was published by the University of Chicago Press. A second book, *The Fragility of Freedom: Tocqueville on Religion, Democracy, and the American Future*, was published in 1995, also by the University of Chicago Press. *Plato's Fable: On the Mortal Condition in Shadowy Times* was published by Princeton University Press in 2006. His most recent book, *Tocqueville in Arabia: Dilemmas in the Democratic Age,* was published by the University of Chicago Press in 2013.

He has recently completed a book entitled *American Awakening: Identity Politics and Other Afflictions of Our Time,* which will be published in 2021.

Dean Nelson

Reverend Dean Nelson serves as the executive director for Human Coalition Action, the advocacy arm of Human Coalition, a national nonprofit organization serving women and families in metropolitan areas. He is also the chairman of the Douglass Leadership Institute, which educates, equips, and empowers minority leaders to bring positive change to their communities.

Rev. Nelson was recently appointed by Maryland Governor Larry Hogan to serve on the congressional Frederick Douglass Bicentennial Commission, whose mission is to honor the life and legacy of Frederick Douglass. He has previously served as the executive director for various nonprofits and has spoken for and worked with a diverse array of groups, including the United Way, NAACP, Prison Fellowship, the SCLC, and TeenPact Leadership Schools. He has appeared on and been published in a variety of media outlets, including MSNBC, ABC, and *USA Today.*

Rev. Nelson and his wife Julia homeschooled their three children, and he has served on the advisory board of the National Black Home Educators. He is a graduate of the University of Virginia.

Clarence Page

Clarence Page, the 1989 Pulitzer Prize winner for commentary, is a columnist syndicated nationally by Tribune Media Services and a member of the *Chicago Tribune*'s editorial board. Page is also a regular contributor of essays to *The News Hour with Jim Lehrer* and has been a regular on *The McLaughlin Group*, NBC's *The Chris Matthews Show*, ABC's *Nightline*, and BET's *Lead Story* news panel programs.

Page's awards include a 1980 Illinois UPI awards for community service for an investigative series titled *The Black Tax* and the Edward Scott Beck Award for overseas reporting in 1976. He also received lifetime achievement awards from the National Society of Newspaper Columnists, the Chicago Headline Club, and the National Association of Black Journalists. In 1992, he was inducted into the Chicago Journalism Hall of Fame.

Page was a reporter, producer, and community affairs director at WBBM-TV from 1980 to 1984. Before that he was a reporter and assistant city editor for the *Chicago Tribune*, during which he participated in a 1972 task force series on vote fraud, which also won a Pulitzer Prize.

His book *Showing My Color: Impolite Essays on Race and Identity* was published in 1996 by Harper Collins.

Page graduated from Ohio University with a bachelor of science in journalism in 1969. He also has received honorary degrees from Columbia College in Chicago, Lake Forest College, the Chicago Theological Seminary, and the John Marshall School of Law, among others.

Page is married, has one son, and lives in the suburbs of Washington, DC.

Wilfred Reilly

Wilfred Reilly is an associate professor of political science at Kentucky State University, a historically black institution. He also teaches courses in the college's intelligence minor, including cyber-security and counter-terrorism. Dr. Reilly is the author, most recently, of the books *Hate Crime Hoax* and *Taboo: Ten Facts You Can't Talk About*. His writing has appeared in publications including *Commentary*, *Quillette*, *USA Today*, the *Washington Times*, and scholarly journals such as *Academic Questions*, in addition to being cited by the *Wall Street Journal*, *Washington Post*, and U.S. Commission on Civil Rights (dissenting report).

Dr. Reilly's academic research interests include international relations, American race relations, the positive and negative impacts of diversity on societies, and the use of modern empirical methods to test "sacred cow" theories. His non-academic interests include cooking, basketball, shooting and archery, and dogs.

Ian Rowe

Ian Rowe is a resident fellow at the American Enterprise Institute, where he focuses on upward mobility, education, family formation, and adoption. Mr. Rowe is a social entrepreneur with more than thirty years of experience founding and leading organizations in the public, private, and nonprofit sectors that empower young people to effect positive change in their own lives.

He is also author of a forthcoming book tentatively entitled *Agency* (Templeton Press), which seeks to inspire young people of all races to build strong families and become masters of their own destiny; cofounder of Vertex Partnership Academies, a new network of character-based, International Baccalaureate high schools opening in the Bronx in 2022; and chairman of the board of Spence-Chapin, one of the nation's premier adoption agencies.

Mr. Rowe concurrently serves as a senior visiting fellow at the Woodson Center, writer for the 1776 Unites campaign, and cofounder of the National Summer School Initiative. Mr. Rowe is the former ten-year CEO of Public Prep, a network of public charter schools educating more than two thousand students in the South Bronx and Lower East Side of Manhattan.

Before joining AEI, Mr. Rowe served as the deputy director of postsecondary success at the Bill & Melinda Gates Foundation; the senior vice president of strategic partnerships and public affairs at MTV, where he won two Public Service Emmy Awards and led campaigns such as Choose or Lose, Fight For Your Rights, and Get Schooled; and the director of strategy and performance measurement at USA Freedom Corps in the White House, overseeing domestic volunteering efforts in the aftermath of 9/11. Mr. Rowe was also part of Teach For America in its early days, where he helped develop a model of assessment that measured teacher effectiveness through student achievement.

Mr. Rowe is a proud product of the New York City public school system. He earned his BS in computer science engineering from Cornell University and his MBA from Harvard Business School, where he was the first black editor-in-chief of the *Harbus*, the Harvard Business School newspaper. Mr. Rowe's work has been published in outlets such as the *Wall Street Journal* and the *Washington Examiner*.

Rev. DeForest Blake Soaries Jr.

Dr. DeForest B. Soaries Jr. is the senior pastor of First Baptist Church of Lincoln Gardens in Somerset, New Jersey. He is the former New Jersey secretary of state and the author of the books *Say Yes to No Debt: 12 Steps to Financial Freedom*, *Meditations for Financial Freedom: Volumes 1&2*, and *Say Yes When Life Says No*. He is the creator of dfree®—a financial freedom movement in use by thousands of churches and organizations across the country.

dfree® has been featured by CNN in a ninety-minute *Black in America* documentary entitled *Almighty Debt*. His work has also been featured in several publications, including the *New York Times*, the *Wall Street Journal*, and *Black Enterprise*.

Dr. Soaries is currently a member of the board of directors at Ocwen Financial Corp. (NYSE: OCN), Independence Realty Trust (NYSE: IRT), and Federal Home Loan Bank of New York. He serves as the compensation chair on all three boards.

Shelby Steele

Shelby Steele is the Robert J. and Marion E. Oster Senior fellow at the Hoover Institution. He specializes in the study of race relations, multiculturalism, and affirmative action. He was appointed a Hoover fellow in 1994.

His first book, *The Content of Our Character: A New Vision of Race in America*, earned Steele a National Book Critics Circle Award (1990). He subsequently wrote a number of books including *White Guilt, A Dream Deferred*, and, most recently, *Shame*.

Steele won an Emmy for his writing on the 1991 documentary *Seven Days in Bensonhurst*. Steele is the recipient of the National Humanities Medal (2004) and the Bradley Prize (2006).

Dr. Carol M. Swain

Dr. Carol M. Swain is the host of the podcast *Be the People* and an author or credited editor of nine books, one of which (*Black Faces, Black Interests*) has won three national awards. Another of her books, *The New White Nationalism in America*, was nominated for a Pulitzer Prize. She is a former university professor of political science and law at Princeton and Vanderbilt universities, and a nationally known political commentator who has appeared on Fox News, ABC Headline News, CNN, BBC Radio, and NPR among other outlets.

Dr. Swain was a Nashville mayoral candidate in 2018 and 2019. Her opinion pieces have been published in the likes of the *New York Times, USA Today, CNN Online*, the *Epoch Times*, the *Washington Post*, and the *Wall Street Journal*.

John Wood Jr.

John Wood Jr. is a national leader and director of public outreach for Braver Angels. A former nominee for Congress, a former vice-chairman of the Republican Party of Los Angeles County, and an adviser on the American Project (an initiative of the Pepperdine School of

Public Policy), John is a noted writer and public speaker on the subjects of moral philosophy and racial and political reconciliation.

His written work has appeared in publications including *Quillette,* the *American Interest, Areo Magazine, Reflections* (a journal of the Yale Divinity School), and RealClearPolicy. His speaking credits include appearances at CPAC, the Global Philanthropy Forum, the Social Capital Summit, the Visionaries Summit, and the Aspen Institute's Weave: The Social Fabric Project. John has also worked in education and youth advocacy in South Los Angeles, where he lives with his wife and three children.

ENDNOTES

1. Frederick Douglass, "What Are the Colored People Doing for Themselves?" (July 14, 1848), in *The Life and Writings of Frederick Douglass*, ed. Philip S. Foner, 4 vols. (New York: International Publishers Co., Inc., 1950), 1:314.

2. Abraham Lincoln, "Letter to Isham Reavis" (November 5, 1855), in *Collected Works of Abraham Lincoln*, ed. Roy P. Basler, 8 vols. (New Brunswick, NJ: Rutgers University Press, 1953–55), 2:327.

3. Abraham Lincoln, "Outline for Speech to the Colonization Society" [January 4, 1855?], *Collected Works*, 2:299, and Second Inaugural Address (March 4, 1865), *Collected Works*, 8:333 ("Yet, if God wills that it continue, until all the wealth piled by the bondman's two hundred and fifty years of unrequited toil shall be sunk, and until every drop of blood drawn with the lash, shall be paid by another drawn with the sword, as was said three thousand years ago, so still it must be said 'the judgments of the Lord, are true and righteous altogether'"); Frederick Douglass, "Lecture on Slavery, No. 1" (December 1, 1850), in *Life and Writings*, 2:133, and ibid., 2:134 ("It has become interwoven with all American institutions, and has anchored itself in the very soil of the American Constitution"). Lincoln records that a "[D]ut[c]h ship carries a cargo of African slaves to Virginia" in 1620, not 1619, whereas Douglass gives no date but says of slavery's introduction to British North America, "The first spot poisoned by its leprous

presence, was a small plantation in Virginia. The slaves, at that time, numbered only twenty."

4   Lincoln put it memorably at Gettysburg, Pennsylvania: "Four score and seven years ago our fathers brought forth on this continent, a new nation, conceived in Liberty, and dedicated to the proposition that all men are created equal." Abraham Lincoln, "Address Delivered at the Dedication of the Cemetery at Gettysburg" (November 19, 1863), *Collected Works*, 7:23. At the invitation of the Rochester Ladies' Anti-Slavery Society, Douglass said to "nearly six hundred white northerners" that the Fourth of July was "the birthday of your National Independence, and of your political freedom." He added, "The 4th of July is the first great fact in your nation's history." Frederick Douglass, "The Meaning of July Fourth for the Negro" (July 5, 1852), in *Life and Writings*, 2:182, 185; David W. Blight, *Frederick Douglass: Prophet of Freedom* (New York, NY: Simon & Schuster, 2018), 236.

5   Douglass, "What Are the Colored People Doing for Themselves?"

6   See Joseph H. Jackson, "Address to the 1964 National Baptist Convention" (1964), *What So Proudly We Hail: The American Soul in Story, Speech, and Song*, ed. Amy A. Kass, Leon R. Kass, and Diana Schaub (Intercollegiate Studies Institute, 2011), online curriculum, https://www.whatsoproudlywehail.org/curriculum/the-american-calendar/address-to-the-1964-national-baptist-convention.

7   Abraham Lincoln, "Speech at Chicago, Illinois" (July 10, 1858), *Collected Works*, 2:499–500.

8   Martin Luther King Jr., "I Have a Dream" (August 28, 1963), in *I Have a Dream: Writings and Speeches that Changed the World*, ed. James Melvin Washington (New York, NY: HarperCollins, 1992), 103.

9   Frederick Douglass, "Our Composite Nationality" (December 7, 1869), in *The Essential Douglass: Selected Writings and Speeches*,

ed. Nicholas Buccola (Indianapolis, IN: Hackett Publishing Company, Inc., 2016), 225.

10 *Plessy v. Ferguson*, 163 U.S. 537 (1896), at 559.

11 *Brown v. Board of Education of Topeka*, 347 U.S. 483 (1954), at 495.

12 For the development of Supreme Court jurisprudence involving race and the equal protection of the laws guaranteed by the Fourteenth Amendment, see Andrew Kull, *The Color-Blind Constitution* (Cambridge, MA: Harvard University Press, 1992).

13 Ibid., 316.

14 Frederick Douglass, "The Nation's Problem" (April 16, 1889), in *African-American Social & Political Thought, 1850–1920*, ed. Howard Brotz and intro. B. William Austin (New Brunswick, NJ: Transaction Publishers, 1992; orig. publ. 1966), 316, 317.

15 Frederick Douglass, "Why Should a Colored Man Enlist?" in *Life and Writings*, 3:341.

16 Frederick Douglass, "The Future of the Negro People of the Slave States" (February 12, 1862), in *Life and Writings*, 3:217.

17 Frederick Douglass, "Reconstruction" (December 1866), in *Life and Writings*, 4:200.

18 From John Adams to Hezekiah Niles (February 13, 1818), Founders Online, National Archives, https://founders.archives. gov/documents/Adams/99-02-02-6854.

19 Frederick Douglass, "The Last Flogging," Chapter XVII of *My Bondage and My Freedom* (1855), in *Essential Douglass*, 19 (emphasis in original).

20 Frederick Douglass, *Narrative of the Life of Frederick Douglass—an American Slave*, ed. Houston A. Baker Jr. (New York: Penguin Books, 1986; orig. publ. 1845), 113.

21 For an account of Lincoln's defense of the American Founding, see Lucas E. Morel, *Lincoln and the American Founding* (Carbondale, IL: Southern Illinois University Press, 2020).

22 Nikole Hannah-Jones, "Our Democracy's Ideals Were False When They Were Written. Black Americans Have Fought to Make Them True," *New York Times Magazine*, August 14, 2019, https://www.nytimes.com/interactive/2019/08/14/magazine/1619-america-slavery.html.

23 See Lucas E. Morel, "America Wasn't Founded on White Supremacy," *American Mind*, October 17, 2019, https://americanmind.org/essays/america-wasnt-founded-on-white-supremacy/.

24 Chamie, Joseph. "Out-of-Wedlock Births Rise Worldwide." YaleGlobal Online, March 16, 2017. Accessed September 2020. https://yaleglobal.yale.edu/content/out-wedlock-births-rise-worldwide.

25 Ibid.

26 Siegel, Fred. *The Future Once Happened Here: New York, D.C., L.A., and the Fate of America's Big Cities.* New York: Encounter Books, 2000.

27 Cohen, Patricia. "What Reparations for Slavery Might Look Like in 2019." *New York Times,* May 23, 2019. Accessed September 2020. https://www.nytimes.com/2019/05/23/business/economy/reparations-slavery.html.

28 Rosin, Hanna. "The Silicon Valley Suicides." *Atlantic,* December 2015. Accessed September 2020. https://www.theatlantic.com/magazine/archive/2015/12/the-silicon-valley-suicides/413140/.

29 Park, Haeyoun, and Matthew Bloch. "How the Epidemic of Drug Overdose Deaths Rippled across America." *New York Times,* January 19, 2016. Accessed 09 2020. https://www.nytimes.com/interactive/2016/01/07/us/drug-overdose-deaths-in-the-us.html.

30 "Morality." Samuel Adams Heritage Society, 2013. Accessed September 2020. http://www.samuel-adams-heritage.com/quotes/morality.html.

31 Oakes, James. *The Scorpion's Sting: Antislavery and the Coming of the Civil War.* New York: W. W. Norton, 2015.

[32] Taylor, Chloe. "Singapore Overtakes the US to Become World's Most Competitive Country, WEF Says." CNBC Make It, October 8, 2019. Accessed October 2020. https://www.cnbc.com/2019/10/08/singapore-overtakes-us-to-become-most-competitive-country-wef-says.html.

[33] Cole, Nicki Lisa. "Defining Racism beyond Its Dictionary Meaning." ThoughtCo, July 14, 2019. Accessed October 2020. https://www.thoughtco.com/racism-definition-3026511.

[34] Avi-Yonah, Shera S. and Molly C. McCafferty. "Asian-American Harvard Admits Earned Highest Average SAT Score of Any Racial Group from 1995 to 2013." *Harvard Crimson,* October 22, 2018. Accessed October 2020. https://www.thecrimson.com/article/2018/10/22/asian-american-admit-sat-scores/.

[35] Bialik, Kristen. "5 Facts about Black Americans." Pew Research Center, February 22, 2018. Accessed September 2020. https://www.pewresearch.org/fact-tank/2018/02/22/5-facts-about-blacks-in-the-u-s/.

[36] DeNavas-Walt, Carmen and Bernadette D. Proctor. "Income and Poverty in the United States: 2014." United States Census Bureau, September 2015. Accessed October 2020. https://www.census.gov/content/dam/Census/library/publications/2015/demo/p60-252.pdf.

[37] Blaustein, Albert P. "Influence of the American Constitution Abroad." Encyclopedia.com, updated December 2020. Accessed September 2020. https://www.encyclopedia.com/politics/encyclopedias-almanacs-transcripts-and-maps/influence-american-constitution-abroad.

[38] Ibid.

39   Pigliucci, Massimo. "Stoicism." Internet Encyclopedia of Philosophy. Accessed September 2020. https://iep.utm.edu/stoicism/.

40   Lazarus, Emma. "The New Colossus." National Park Service, updated August 14, 2019. Accessed September 2020. https://www.nps.gov/stli/learn/historyculture/colossus.htm.

41   Obama, Barack. "Barack Obama's Speech on Race." *New York Times*, March 18, 2018. Accessed September 14, 2020. https://www.nytimes.com/2008/03/18/us/politics/18text-obama.html.

42   Ibid.

43   Hannah-Jones, Nikole. "The 1619 Project." *New York Times Magazine*, August 14, 2019. Accessed 2020. https://www.nytimes.com/interactive/2019/08/14/magazine/1619-america-slavery.html?.

44   Coates, Ta-Nehisi. "The Case for Reparations." *Atlantic*, 2014. Accessed 09 2020. https://www.theatlantic.com/magazine/archive/2014/06/the-case-for-reparations/361631/.

45   Ibid.

46   Gross, Terry. "A 'Forgotten History' of How the U.S. Government Segregated America." NPR, May 3, 2017. Accessed 09 2020. https://www.npr.org/2017/05/03/526655831/a-forgotten-history-of-how-the-u-s-government-segregated-america.

47   Grady, Denise. "White Doctors, Black Subjects: Abuse Disguised as Research." *New York Times*, January 23, 2007. Accessed 09 2020. https://www.nytimes.com/2007/01/23/health/23book.html.

48   History.com editors. "Great Society." History.com, updated August 28, 2018. Accessed September 2020. https://www.history.com/topics/1960s/great-society.

49   Hughes, Coleman. "The Racism Treadmill." *Quillette*, May 14, 2018. Accessed September 2020. https://quillette.com/2018/05/14/the-racism-treadmill/.

50 Gates Jr., Henry Louis. *The Classic Slave Narratives.* New York: Signet, 2012.

51 Hannah-Jones. "The 1619 Project."

52 C-Span. "Hillary Clinton on 'Superpredators.'" YouTube video, 02:02. February 25, 2016. Accessed September 2020. https://www.youtube.com/watch?v=j0uCrA7ePno.

53 Sullivan, Ali, and Zach Rosenthal. "Nikole Hannah-Jones — Creator of the 1619 Project — Speaks at the Rotunda, the Haven." *Cavalier Daily,* February 19, 2020. Accessed September 2020. https://www.cavalierdaily.com/article/2020/02/nikole-hannah-jones-creator-of-the-1619-project-speaks-at-the-rotunda-the-haven.

54 Coates. "The Case for Reparations."

55 Hughes, Coleman. "My Testimony on Reparations." *Quillette,* June 20, 2019. Accessed September 2020. https://quillette.com/2019/06/20/my-testimony-to-congress-on-reparations/.

56 Bittker, Boris I. *The Case for Black Reparations.* New York: Beacon Press, (1972) 2003.

57 Robinson, Randall. *The Debt: What America Owes to Blacks.* New York: Plume, 2000.

58 NBC New York. "Democratic Debate: Amy Klobuchar: 'That's What We Call at Home 'All Foam and No Beer' | NBC New York." YouTube video, 00:30. June 26, 2019. Accessed September 2020. https://www.youtube.com/watch?v=COJY5tROdq0.

59 Buck, Stuart. *Acting White: The Ironic Legacy of Desegragation.* New Haven: Yale University Press, 2012.

60 Cose, Ellis. *The Rage of a Privileged Class: Why Do Prosperous Blacks Still Have the Blues?* New York: HarperCollins, 2006.

61 Rustin, Bayard. "From Protest to Politics: The Future of the Civil Rights Movement." BlackPast, June 18, 2017. Accessed September 2020. https://www.blackpast.org/african-american-history/1965-bayard-rustin-protest-politics-future-civil-rights-movement-0/.

62   Cole, Rhea. "Slaveholding in Northern States." American Civil War Forum, 2016. Accessed September 2020. https://www.americancivilwarforum.com/slaveholding-in-northern-states-1480.html.

63   Williams, Walter E. "The True Black Tragedy." Creators.com, May 20, 2015. Accessed September 2020. https://www.creators.com/read/walter-williams/05/15/the-true-black-tragedy.

64   Wikipedia. S.v. "Slavery in Ancient Greece." Updated December 2, 2020. Accessed September 2020. https://en.wikipedia.org/wiki/Slavery_in_ancient_Greece.

65   Hannah-Jones. "The 1619 Project."

66   United States Census Bureau. "1790 Overview." Updated December 17, 2019. Accessed September 2020. https://www.census.gov/history/www/through_the_decades/overview/1790.html.

67   Schulman, Marc. "Economics and the Civil War." History Central. Accessed September 2020. https://www.historycentral.com/CivilWar/AMERICA/Economics.html.

68   Sowell, Thomas. *Black Rednecks and White Liberals.* New York: Encounter Books, 2009.

69   Phillips, Matt. "The Long Story of U.S. Debt, From 1790 to 2011, in 1 Little Chart." *Atlantic,* November 13, 2020. Accessed September 2020. https://www.theatlantic.com/business/archive/2012/11/the-long-story-of-us-debt-from-1790-to-2011-in-1-little-chart/265185/.

70   Cohen, Jennie. "Civil War Deadlier than Previously Thought." History.com, updated August 13, 2018. Accessed September 2020. https://www.history.com/news/civil-war-deadlier-than-previously-thought.

71   Williams. "The True Black Tragedy."

72   Reilly, Wilfred. *Taboo: Ten Facts You Can't Talk About.* Washington, DC: Regnery Publishing, 2020.

73 Coleman, Nancy. "Why We're Capitalizing Black." *New York Times,* July 5, 2020. Accessed September 2020. https://www.nytimes.com/2020/07/05/insider/capitalized-black.html.

74 Associated Press. "AP Changes Writing Style to Capitalize "B" in Black." June 19, 2020. Accessed September 2020. https://apnews.com/article/71386b46dbff8190e71493a763e8f45a.

75 Willis, Kim. "Beyoncé Unveils Longer Trailer for Visual Album '*Black Is King*' and Twitter Goes Bonkers." *USA Today,* updated June 29, 2020. Accessed September 2020. https://www.usatoday.com/story/entertainment/music/2020/06/28/beyonce-teases-black-is-king-new-visual-album-heading-disney/3274547001/.

76 Byrd, Robert. "Oprah Winfrey Brings Her Show to Forsyth County." Associated Press, February 9, 1987. Accessed September 2020. https://apnews.com/article/ba34b1912707682f6bcd4a88251c29a8.

77 Ali, Abdullah Yusuf. *The Meaning of the Holy Qu'ran,* English, Arabic and Arabic edition. Beltsville, MD: Amana Publications, 2006.

78 UPROXX Video. "N.W.A., King Tee, Ice-T, MC Hammer, Tone-Loc, etc. - We're All in the Same Gang." YouTube video, 05:07. July 13, 2012. Accessed September 2020. https://www.youtube.com/watch?v=Pmg6c0PASYk.

79 UPROXX Video. "BDP, Stetsasonic, Kool Moe Dee, MC Lyte, Doug Fresh, Just-Ice, Heavy D, Chuck D - Self Destruction." YouTube video, 06:01. November 27, 2011. Accessed September 2020. https://www.youtube.com/watch?v=MmX5TgWsfEQ.

80 BoogieDwnProdVEVO. "Boogie Down Productions - Love's Gonna Get'cha (Material Love)."
YouTube video, 04:57. January 25, 2018. Accessed September 2020. https://www.youtube.com/watch?v=4NACMjwR5DE

81 Obama, Barrack. "Transcript: Obama's Commencement Speech at Morehouse College." *Wall Street Journal,* May 20, 2013. Accessed 09 2020. https://blogs.wsj.com/washwire/2013/05/20/

transcript-obamas-commencement-speech-at-morehouse-college/.

82 Young, Damon. "The Definition, Danger and Disease of Respectability Politics, Explained." Root, March 21, 2016. Accessed September 2020. https://www.theroot.com/the-definition-danger-and-disease-of-respectability-po-1790854699.

83 Dilbeck, D. H. "The Radical Christian Faith of Frederick Douglass." *Christianity Today*, December 21, 2017. Accessed September 2020. https://www.christianitytoday.com/ct/2018/january-february/frederick-douglass-at-200-remembering-his-radical-christian.html.

84 Gudmestad, Robert. "Faith Made Harriet Tubman Fearless as She Rescued Slaves." Conversation, December 3, 2019. Accessed September 2020. https://theconversation.com/faith-made-harriet-tubman-fearless-as-she-rescued-slaves-127592.

85 "The Life and Theories of Marcus Garvey." Michigan State University. Accessed September 2020. https://msu.edu/user/h/a/harri283/web/112/sarahp.htm.

86 "Malcolm X Organization of Afro-American Unity." *New York Times*, August 10, 1964. Accessed September 2020. https://www.nytimes.com/1964/08/10/archives/malcolm-x-organization-of-afroamerican-unity.html.

87 Muhammad, Masjid. "The Late, Iman WD Mohammed." Nation's Mosque, October 6, 2013. Accessed September 2020. https://thenationsmosque.org/about/the-late-imam-wd-mohammed/.

88 Muhammad, Imam W. Deen. "Remove All Images from Worship." *A. M. Journal*, May 27, 1983. Accessed 09 2020. http://www.newafricaradio.com/articles/5-27-83.html.

89 National Archives. "Founders Letters." September 17, 2020. Accessed October 2020. https://founders.archives.gov/.

90 Hannah-Jones. "The 1619 Project."

91 "Declaration of Independence: A Transcription." National Archives. Last reviewed July 24, 2020. Accessed October 2020. https://www.archives.gov/founding-docs/declaration-transcript.

92 "Home." Project H.O.O.D., 2020. Accessed October 2020. https://www.projecthood.org/.

93 Desmond, Matthew. "In Order to Understand the Brutality of American Capitalism, You Have to Start on the Plantation." *New York Times Magazine.* August 14, 2019. Accessed October 2020. https://www.nytimes.com/interactive/2019/08/14/magazine/slavery-capitalism.html.

94 Elkins, Stanley. *Slavery: A Problem in American Institutional and Intellectual Life.* Chicago: University of Chicago Press, 1976.

95 Puhak, Shelley. "The Abuses of Enchantment." *National Journal of Literature,* September 3, 2019. Accessed October 2020. https://www.vqronline.org/essays-articles/2019/09/abuses-enchantment.

96 Stampp, Kenneth. *The Peculiar Institution: Slavery in the Ante-Bellum South.* New York: Vintage, 1976.

97 Ibid.

98 Hill, Herbert. "The Problem of Race in American Labor History." *Reviews in American History* 4, no. 2 (1996): 189–208. https://www.jstor.org/stable/30030646?seq=1.

99 Innes, Wendy. "Work Ethic: Is It a Race or Ethnicity Issue?" USAonRace, October 4, 2010. Accessed October 2020. https://www.usaonrace.com/cover-stories/1699/work-ethic-is-it-a-race-or-ethnicity-issue.html.

100 Wesley, Charles. *Negro Labor in the United States, 1850–1925: A Study in American Economic History.* New York: Vanguard Press, 1927.

101 DuBois, W. E. B. *The Negro Artisan. Report of a Social Study Made under the Direction of Atlanta University.* Atlanta, GA: Atlanta University Press, May 27, 1902. Internet Archive. https://archive.org/details/negroartisanrepo07dubo/page/n6/mode/2up.

102 Rothstein, Richard. "The Urban Poor Shall Inherit Poverty." *American Prospect,* January 7, 2014. Accessed October 2020. https://prospect.org/education/urban-poor-shall-inherit-poverty/.

103 Coates, Ta-Nehisi. *The Beautiful Struggle.* New York: One World Publishing, 2009.

104 Collins, Patricia Hill. "New Commodities, New Consumers: Selling Blackness in a Global Marketplace." *Ethnicities* 6, no. 3 (September 2006): 297–317. https://journals.sagepub.com/doi/10.1177/1468796806068322.

105 Furstenberg Jr., Frank F., et al. "Race Differences in the Timing of Adolescent Intercourse." *American Sociological Review* 52, no. 4 (1987): 511–518. https://www.jstor.org/stable/2095296?seq=1.

106 Cherry, Robert, and Chun Wang. "Labor Market Conditions and US Teen Birth Rates, 2001–2009." *Journal of Family and Economic Issues* 36, no. 3 (2015): 408–420. https://link.springer.com/article/10.1007/s10834-014-9402-7.

107 Kearney, Melissa S., and Phillip B. Levin. "Why Is the Teen Birth Rate in the United States So High and Why Does It Matter?" National Poverty Center, June 2012. Accessed October 2020. http://npc.umich.edu/publications/u/2012-15-NPC-Working-Paper.pdf.

108 Kearney, Melissa S. and Phillip B. Levine. "Early Non-Marital Childbearing and the 'Culture of Despair.'" Legacy Papers, April 8, 2011. Accessed October 2020.
http://papers.economics.ubc.ca/legacypapers/kearney.pdf.

109 Centers for Disease Control and Prevention. "Teen Birth Rates Fall Nearly 50 Percent among Hispanic and Black Teens, Dropping National Teen Birth Rate to an All-Time Low." CDC Newsroom, last reviewed April 28, 2016. Accessed October 2020. https://www.cdc.gov/media/releases/2016/p0428-teen-birth-rates.html.

110 National Center for Education Statistics. "Percentage of Persons 25 to 29 Years Old with Selected
Levels of Educational Attainment, by Race/Ethnicity and Sex: Selected Years, 1920 through 2017." Digest of Education Statistics. Accessed October 2020. https://nces.ed.gov/programs/digest/d17/tables/dt17_104.20.asp.

111 Hurst, Roy. "Stepin Fetchit, Hollywood's First Black Film Star." NPR, March 6, 2006. Accessed October 2020. https://www.npr.org/templates/story/story.php?storyId=5245089.

112 Wikipedia. S.v. "Reparations for Slavery." Last edited December 14, 2020. Accessed October 2020. https://en.wikipedia.org/wiki/Reparations_for_slavery.

113 Anti-Slavery International. "Tony Blair Apologies [sic] for Britain's Role in the Slave Trade." March 15, 2007. Accessed October 2020. https://www.antislavery.org/tony-blair-apologies-britains-role-slave-trade-2/.

114 Tanner, Michael. "What's Missing in the War on Poverty?" Cato Institute, January 23, 2019. Accessed October 2020. https://www.cato.org/publications/commentary/whats-missing-war-poverty.

115 Kids Count Data Center. "Children in Single-Parent Families by Race in the United States." Updated January 2020. Accessed October 2020. https://datacenter.kidscount.org/data/tables/107-children-in-single-parent-families-by-race#detailed/1/any/false/867,133,38,35,18/10,9,12,1,185,13/432,431.

116 I am proud to say that my own Black History Month presentations have improved considerably from the time I stood holding up a hand-drawn poster depicting slaves fleeing servitude on the back of a pickup truck.

117 Martin Luther King, Jr. Research and Education Institute. "March on Washington for Jobs and Freedom. Accessed October 2020. https://kinginstitute.stanford.edu/encyclopedia/march-washington-jobs-and-freedom#:~:text=The%20march%20

was%20successful%20in,on%20Washington%20had%20
several%20precedents.

[118] Military Hall of Honor. "Col William Hayward." Accessed
October 2020. https://militaryhallofhonor.com/honoree-record.
php?id=2619.

[119] Keyes, Allison. "The East St. Louis Race Riot Left Dozens Dead,
Devastating a Community on the Rise." *Smithsonian Magazine.*
June 30, 2017. Accessed October 2020.
https://www.smithsonianmag.com/smithsonian-institution/east-
st-louis-race-riot-left-dozens-dead-devastating-community-on-
the-rise-180963885/.

[120] Gonzalez, Michelle. "Black History Month: Highlighting the
93rd Division in World War I." National Guard, February 10,
2016. Accessed October 2020. https://www.nationalguard.mil/
News/Article/653966/black-history-month-highlighting-the-
93rd-division-in-world-war-i/.

[121] Jordan, William G. *Black Newspapers and America's War for
Democracy, 1914–1920.* Chapel Hill: University of North Carolina
Press, 2003.

[122] Army.mil. "Medal of Honor: Seargent Henry Johnson." Accessed
October 2020. https://www.army.mil/medalofhonor/johnson/.

[123] Matthews, Dylan. "Everything You Need to Know about the War on
Poverty." *Washington Post,* January 8, 2014. Accessed October 2020.
https://www.washingtonpost.com/news/wonk/wp/2014/01/08/
everything-you-need-to-know-about-the-war-on-poverty/.

[124] Vance, J. D. *Hillbilly Elegy: A Memoir of a Family and Culture in
Crisis.* New York: Harper, 2016.

[125] Wilson, William Julius. *When Work Disappears: The World of the
New Urban Poor.* New York: Vintage, 1997.

[126] Seligman, Martin E. P. "Learned Helplessness." University of
Pennsylvania, 1972. Accessed October 2020. https://ppc.sas.
upenn.edu/sites/default/files/learnedhelplessness.pdf.

127 King Jr., Martin Luther. "Where Do We Go from Here?" Speech, Atlanta, GA, August 16, 1967. Martin Luther King, Jr., Research and Education Institute. Accessed October 2020. https://kinginstitute.stanford.edu/king-papers/documents/where-do-we-go-here-address-delivered-eleventh-annual-sclc-convention.

128 King Jr., Martin Luther. "I Have a Dream." Speech, Washington, DC, August 28, 1963. Martin Luther King, Jr., Research and Education Institute. Accessed October 2020. https://kinginstitute.stanford.edu/king-papers/documents/i-have-dream-address-delivered-march-washington-jobs-and-freedom.

129 Sullivan, Andrew. "The Speech." *Atlantic*, March 18, 2008. Accessed October 2020. https://www.theatlantic.com/daily-dish/archive/2008/03/the-speech/218808/.

130 Obama, Barack. "A More Perfect Union." Speech, Philadelphia, PA, March 18, 2008. National Constitution Center. Accessed October 2020. https://constitutioncenter.org/amoreperfectunion/.

131 Allen, Erin. "How Did America Get Its Name?" Library of Congress, July 4, 2016. Accessed October 2020. https://blogs.loc.gov/loc/2016/07/how-did-america-get-its-name/.

132 Library of Congress. "Exploring the Early Americas." Accessed October 2020. https://www.loc.gov/exhibits/exploring-the-early-americas/.

133 Hannah-Jones. "The 1619 Project."

134 Jesuthasan, Meerabelle. "The 1619 Project Sparks Dialogue and Reflection in Schools Nationwide." Pulitzer Center, December 20, 2019. Accessed October 2020. https://pulitzercenter.org/blog/1619-project-sparks-dialogue-and-reflection-schools-nationwide.

135 Hannah-Jones. "The 1619 Project."

136 *Karen Hunter Show*. "Nikole Hannah-Jones on Reparations." YouTube video, 06:54. December 10, 2019. https://www.youtube.com/watch?v=w4m4aOF2xYs&feature=youtu.be.

137 Owens, Burgess. "I Didn't Earn Slavery Reparations, and I Don't Want Them." *Wall Street Journal*, May 24, 2019. Accessed October 2020. https://www.wsj.com/articles/i-didnt-earn-slavery-reparations-and-i-dont-want-them-11558732429.

138 Chetty, Raj, et al. "Where is the Land of Opportunity?" Opportunity Insights, January 2014. Accessed October 2020. https://opportunityinsights.org/wp-content/uploads/2018/03/Geography-Executive-Summary-and-Memo-January-2014-1.pdf.

139 Wilcox, W. Bradford. "The Millennial Success Sequence: Marriage, Kids, and the 'Success Sequence' among Young Adults." American Enterprise Institute, June 14, 2017. Accessed October 2020. https://www.aei.org/research-products/working-paper/millennials-and-the-success-sequence-how-do-education-work-and-marriage-affect-poverty-and-financial-success-among-millennials/.

140 Wilcox, W. Bradford. "Black Men Making It in America: The Engines of Economic Success for Black Men in America." American Enterprise Institute, June 26, 2018. Accessed October 2020. https://www.aei.org/research-products/report/black-men-making-it-in-america-the-engines-of-economic-success-for-black-men-in-america/.

141 Hannah-Jones, Nikole. "Choosing a School for My Daughter in a Segregated City." *New York Times,* June 9, 2016. Accessed October 2020. https://www.nytimes.com/2016/06/12/magazine/choosing-a-school-for-my-daughter-in-a-segregated-city.html.

142 *Amanpour & Company*. "Nikole Hannah-Jones Discusses Busing and Desegregation." PBS video, 19:03. August 2, 2019. Accessed October 2020. http://www.pbs.org/wnet/amanpour-and-company/video/nikole-hannah-jones-discusses-busing-and-desegregation/.

143 Hertzberg, Hendrik and Henry Louis Gates Jr. "The African-American Century." *New Yorker Magazine,* April 22, 1996.

Accessed October 2020. https://www.newyorker.com/magazine/1996/04/29/the-african-american-century.

144 Obama. "A More Perfect Union."

145 National Trust for Historic Preservation. "Rosenwald Schools." Accessed October 2020. https://savingplaces.org/places/rosenwald-schools#.X4Rx3hrsvud.

146 Blight, David W. *Frederick Douglass: Prophet of Freedom.* New York: Simon & Schuster, 2018.

147 Weber, Max. *The Protestant Ethic and the Spirit of Capitalism: And Other Writings.* New York: Penguin, 2002.

148 Bernardo, Joseph. "Natonal Negro Business League." BlackPast. November 26, 2008. Accessed October 2020. https://www.blackpast.org/african-american-history/national-negro-business-league/.

149 Hipple, Stephen F. and Laurel A. Hammond. "Self-Employment in the United States." U.S. Bureau of Labor Statistics, March 2016. Accessed October 2020. https://www.bls.gov/spotlight/2016/self-employment-in-the-united-states/pdf/self-employment-in-the-united-states.pdf.

150 History.com editors. "Black Codes." History.com, updated October 10, 2019. Accessed October 2020. https://www.history.com/topics/black-history/black-codes.

151 Hardin, Robin, and Marcie Hinton. 2001. "The Squelching of Free Speech in Memphis: The Life of a Black Post-Reconstruction Newspaper." *Race, Gender, & Class Journal* 8, no. 4 (2001): 78–95. https://www.jstor.org/stable/41674996.

152 Buck, Stuart. *Acting White: The Ironic Legacy of De-Segregation.* New Haven, CT: Yale University Press, 2010, 45–50.

153 Cowen, Tyler. *The Complacent Class: The Self-Defeating Quest for the American Dream.* London: Picador, 2017, 28–30.

154 Hoffer, Eric. *The Temper of Our Time.* New Jersey: Hopewell Publications, 2008.

155 Steele, Shelby. *Shame: How America's Past Sins Have Polarized Our Country.* New York: Basic Books, 2015.

156 Murawski, John. "'1619 Project' Already Shaping Schoolkids' Minds on Race." RealClearPolitics, January 20, 2020. Accessed October 2020. https://www.realclearpolitics.com/2020/01/30/1619_project_already_shaping_schoolkids_minds_on_race_499773.html.

157 Silverstein, Jake. "Why We Published the 1619 Project." *New York Times Magazine,* December 20, 2019. Accessed October 2020. https://www.nytimes.com/interactive/2019/12/20/magazine/1619-intro.html.

ACKNOWLEDGMENTS

This book would not have been possible without the help and support of countless devoted individuals. I am indebted to our core 1776 Unites launch team, led by Beth Feeley, Dan Proft, Terence Mathis, and Sandy Tolliver. I am also deeply grateful to Maria Brazda, Collette Caprara, Hattie Porterfield, Curtis Watkins, and the entire Woodson Center staff. And of course, none of this would have happened without the "early adopters"—key supporters who invested in this initiative when it was only an idea: Jim Forrest, Greg Kunes, Phil and Marsha Dowd, Scott Mitchell, Bill Myers, Richard Watts, Berni Neal, and others. Thank you all.

Made in the USA
Monee, IL
26 May 2021